The World Comes to Alameda

The World Comes to Alameda

Life Stories by Members of Mastick Senior
Center in Alameda, California

Mastick Senior Center

ISBN-13: 9781978181847
ISBN-10: 1978181841
Library of Congress Control Number: 2017916199
CreateSpace Independent Publishing Platform
North Charleston, South Carolina

Table of Contents

Preface

Mastick Senior Center

Mastick Senior Center was named after Edwin Baird Mastick, one of California's first attorneys and a longtime Alamedan. Born in Ohio in 1824, Mastick studied law and taught school before coming west. He settled in Alameda with his wife and children in 1864, practiced law in San Francisco, and served as clerk of the state supreme court. As president of the Alameda board of city trustees for nine years, Mastick led the city to implement several important infrastructure projects.

After Mastick's death in 1901, Encinal Elementary School was renamed in his honor. The original three-story building was demolished in 1937 and replaced with the current single-story structure. Mastick Elementary remained in operation until 1980, when it was closed as a part of a school-consolidation plan. The school district then leased the site to the city for use as a senior center, which also took Mastick's name. In its first year of operation, Mastick Senior Center provided services and programs for more than four hundred members; twelve years later, in 1992, the center was recognized by the California Department of Aging for a comprehensive range of services, programs, and activities for some twenty-five hundred members. The school district conveyed the property to the city in 2000.

In 2017 Mastick Senior Center is alive and well. A division of the City of Alameda Recreation and Parks Department, Mastick is open six days a week and offers nearly one hundred classes, a program of day trips and extended travel, and numerous services and resources, all supported by more than two hundred volunteers, the center's successful fundraising efforts, and the City of Alameda. This memoir project originated as one member's aspiration and was realized by the collaborative effort of the center's staff, volunteers, membership, and advisory board, a simple but eloquent expression of Mastick Senior Center at its best.

The pieces in this book range from straightforward life summaries to accounts of memorable episodes and poems capturing a moment or period in the writer's life. Together they are a sampler of the array of experience that can be found among any group of people. Joy, sorrow, and triumph are felt by people of every culture and creed. We are truly more alike than unalike. And as these stories reveal, it is also our uniqueness that makes us a whole—a whole community, a whole world.

Information about E. B. Mastick from Woodruff Minor, *Alameda at Play: A Century of Public Parks and Recreation in Alameda from the Victorian Era to the Present Day* (Alameda, CA: ARPD / Friends of the Parks, Inc. Alameda, 2001, 118–19).

As I Remember Things

Mary Ashford

Joan and John, 1937

It's my favorite photo of my parents:
posing in their Sunday best, her silk dress
and trendy bob, his sporty plus-fours,
both of them hoping that things turn out well.

It's before she resorted to slow, white burn,
freezing him out like a long winter.
It's before the pink spots of the British Empire
disappeared from the map of the world.

It's before a nip turned into a pint,
before the sound of his key at the door
sent five of their six daughters running away
to distant parts of the Commonwealth.

Paddington Station, 1943

Five years old:

and lost at Paddington Station, scanning the crowd for a sight of the dad who had disappeared among the porters jostling for tips, coppers on the beat, uniformed soldiers, sailors, airmen, all rushing to the hiss of giant locomotives, and harried rush-hour workers heading for a grubby steamed-up coffee shop serving wartime fare like bread and dripping, bubble and squeak, jam tarts and black stewed tea. Perhaps Dad had gone off to buy a pack of ten fags or to find a bookie to put two bob on a Newmarket filly. I never asked him why he hid behind a pillar to watch me run around wildly in terror. I never asked him why he was laughing. We left the station in silence through thick fog, the smell of hot greasy cooking fat, and newly bomb-damaged buildings. We were at war.

The Reader, late 1940s

What would she give to ride to school at the top of an old double-decker with a cheeky cockney conductor taking fares and keeping kids in order, and then stop off at the local library on the way home.

What would she give to spend time cross-legged on the carpeted floor of the children's room, reading a story retold from Shakespeare or Dickens, and walking home with a stack of books under her arm.

What would she give for her dreams to be as modest as they were then: suspense, delight, and happy endings for the likes of Davey Copperfield and Oliver Twist unfolding on foggy London evenings after tea.

Saturday Morning Pictures, 1940s

Side by side through foggy lanes, our pockets holding a sixpence to get in and a penny for sweets, me and my sister would walk to the shabby local cinema our mother labeled the bughouse and settle into hard, wonky ripped seats. Saturday Morning Pictures lasted about two hours and opened with a short Western, usually "goodies" (cowboys) hunting the "baddies" (Indians) through stark rocky terrain. The kids around us were mostly Londoners, cockneys, Protestants in name if not in practice, from the local elementary. We were in the minority, Scots-Welsh Catholics attending a fee-paying private Catholic school in a nearby town, where 50 percent of the students were Jewish or foreign-born. But for two hours every Saturday we were all one, waving at the screen, screaming at the cowboys to look behind the boulder where the large white-feathered tip of a tribal warbonnet peeked from the black-and-white landscape. "He's right behind you!" rang out in unison. The cowboy picture was followed by a live talent show, leaving me with scant memories of pop singers and lots of tap dancers. A cartoon ended the program. The old cinema did better in the 60s when technicolor came out. It then became a bingo hall, before it finally closed altogether. By then most of my sisters had flown the coop for greener pastures.

I Wanted My Dreams to Be Blue, circa 1952

At Catholic school the mood was somber,
like our chestnut winter uniforms and the
dark-brown habits of the nuns.
On school outings in spring, our matching
teal dresses prompted local ruffians
to mock: "We like the one in blue!"

My favorite colors are shades of blue:
cornflower, sapphire, cobalt, royal, sky.
"English girls don't pierce their ears,"
scolded one nun, seizing my new blue studs.
"We must excuse your friend Maria, she's Italian."
How I longed to be Italian, to sing opera, to talk
with my hands, to use a lovely word like *azzurro*,
to imagine Prince Charming even more romantically
by his Italian name, *Il principe azzurro.*

As Told to My Grandson

This is what I remember:
It was 1962, and I was twenty-four.
My boyfriend had left me.
I thought of going to America
as a great adventure.
I promised I'd be gone
for no more than a year.
Getting a green card took two hours
at the US embassy in London.

It took three days to get a job
in Chicago. I met your grandpa
on my first day at work.
I earned about $4,200 a year.
A studio apartment cost $85 a month.
A flight to my aunts in Los Angeles cost $35.
Mail took about a week to the UK
from the US, and my parents waited
impatiently for my letters home.
John F. Kennedy was president.
It was the era known as Camelot.

The Garden

Janet Beatty

When I was around ten years old I was required on Saturday mornings to learn how to iron handkerchiefs and pillowcases, and later, my own skirts and blouses. I would stand at the ironing board, tutored by my mother as she did the weekly laundry. Someday, my mother said, I would understand how important it was to do my ironing correctly. Later in the day I would be at the piano, putting in my daily hour of practice, my hands, patiently, boringly running up and down the keys in variations of scales. Someday when I was better and could play actual songs, I would be grateful, my mother said. Ironing and music, along with learning to cook and keep house, were valuable gifts every girl should have. I hated these chores even as I accepted them.

Meanwhile, my older brother was outside in the sunshine, mowing the lawn and weeding under my mother's rosebushes. Important tasks every boy should learn, my mother said. I was jealous of his kind of chores.

Every year when school was out for the summer, my brother and I were shipped off to spend a couple of months with our mother's brother, my Uncle Harold, and Aunt Esther and their five children, most of whom were much younger than me. My aunt and uncle were poor—the family was crammed into a tiny house and had only one old car. The kids wore hand-me-down clothes, often from my brother and me. They lived in a very small town in the Palouse hills of eastern Washington. All around were farms and ranches and endless fields of ripening summer wheat. Some of the town's streets were not paved. All of us children were expected to be outside all day, playing. We would go down to the Touchet River and hunt for pollywogs. We ran barefoot through the nearby pasture, being careful not to get too close to the cows and geese. We got filthy dirty and tore the knees out of our pants. And none of the grown-ups seemed to care. I eagerly looked forward to our summers there.

Every spring, to supplement Uncle Harold's meager income, Aunt Esther planted a huge garden. My mother was disdainful of letting me get dirty. But Aunt Esther invited me into the garden and while the younger children napped began to show me the wonders there: This was a corn tassel and that was the corn silk and here was how the silks were fertilized to create ears of corn. Here were rows and rows of beets and carrots and potatoes, which grew hidden beneath the dirt. Aunt Esther introduced me to kohlrabi and taught me how to pick through the lettuce and search for snails. I learned how to stake tomato plants and build a string trellis for peas. As my aunt and I dug and planted and weeded, I discovered the joy of getting my hands into the soil.

While the other kids scattered throughout the neighborhood, off on adventures of their own, I would help my aunt harvest. After we brought the vegetables into the house, she showed me how to clean, cook, and store them. In the storeroom off the kitchen, jars of applesauce and raspberry jam lined the shelves. Packages of fresh vegetables filled the freezer.

I would go home at summer's end and pick up my iron, play the piano, and help my mother cook. Any attempt to convince her to let me grow something other than roses was met with flat refusal. It wasn't appropriate for a young lady to dig in the dirt. That was men's work. She explained that as a growing young woman, I must learn the proper role of wife, mother, and friend. And do it with clean hands.

And so it went until I was grown. After I left my mother's house, wherever I lived I dug up the earth and planted vegetables. When I moved to Alameda, I lived in an apartment for the first time, and there was nowhere to dig in the dirt. Then I discovered the Bay/Eagle Community Garden and for the next fifteen years managed to grow vegetables and herbs there. My two daughters, long steeped in the joy of gardening, reaped the bounty of my work. And now I have brought my grandchildren into the garden to learn how to get really dirty, search for wiggly worms or snails, and discover where food comes from. I plant corn, beans, tomatoes, carrots, beets, cucumbers, summer squash and, of course, kohlrabi. What we can't eat or preserve goes to the Alameda City Food Bank.

Beyond the joy of growing and eating my own food, my garden is a refuge, a place of quiet contemplation or to not think about anything at all. Other gardeners bring their iPods with music or podcasts, or a radio to follow the never-ending political news. I want to tune all that out there, to just be still with the plants and the weeds and the silent beauty of growing things.

My mother would have been appalled by my passion for gardening, for pesticide-free vegetables, for canning and freezing food for the winter. She would probably "tut tut" at my cracked, mud-encrusted fingernails and filthy jeans. Aunt Esther, however, would have been proud.

Someone Only a Lover Could Mother

Bonnie Bone

Trying to help my little brother, Marty, remains one of the hardest, most psychically damaging endeavors I've attempted in my life. I know needy people often strike out at those closest to them, those trying to help them. I knew Marty felt– and I didn't disagree—that health-wise, he had been dealt a bad hand. And I knew he'd been brought up to expect a loyal woman to marry him and care for him until he died, like our mother had our dad. But Marty was a local rock star—a Fender man, Stratocaster—and his own loyalty was to himself and to his music: the two were not separable. While generally private and reserved, Marty was funny and witty around his friends. He is sensitive and intelligent—but moody, very moody. And even though I may have been his favorite living sister, I was not his favorite person—not even in his top fifty. And, for all my sisterly assistance, I was not a wife, nor a girlfriend nor even a devoted fan—and I believe he resented that: that it was I who was helping him because he had no one else—particularly after our mother passed away. And, as a sister—a tired, busy professional with no family of her own, who perhaps resented that her only "child" was her brother—I'm sure I was probably more Nurse Ratchett to him than the caring attendant our mom had always been to our dad.

My brother's independence began to slip away from him while he was living in a charming little ramshackle he owned near Dogwood Drive in the same small town we had grown up in. He made his living repairing sound equipment for a business owned by longtime friends, and he played paying gigs on the weekends throughout the Atlanta area. Back then, he also sold a little pot on the side, but mostly it was for his own consumption. Then he began suffering from long, debilitating bouts of depression and from unexplained seizures that caused him to suddenly lose all motor control and collapse paralyzed onto the ground where he often hurt himself, and from where he would be forced to observe, as well as endure, the humiliating aftermath of public alarm while he was unable to move even his eyeballs. He began to spend more and more time within the safe confines of his little home.

About this same time, other aspects of my little brother's world also began to crumble about him. The ever-expanding Atlanta airport had decimated our town, the Ford plant there had closed, several local airlines had gone out of business, and our idyllic—if parochial—little hometown became somewhat of a depressed area with its attendant rise in joblessness creating a rise in poverty and in petty crime as well. The population and the demographics of our hometown were changing too. Instead of being hailed and honked at by friends on his daily walk to the Qwik-Pik for cigarettes, my brother—a lean six-foot-three with brown hair down to his waist—would sometimes be mocked and called "Willie" by people gathered around the convenience store, people he did not know. His home, where he stored musical and sound equipment he was working on for resale, was twice broken into. He had no health insurance, and the frequent, mysterious seizures—plus his own failure to convert his repair skills from analog to digital—resulted in his inability to keep a job in the only field of work that he knew. And just as he was struggling to keep up with his bills and his mortgage, he was arrested for selling pot. He successfully completed a pretrial diversion program and his arrest was expunged; but compliance with the terms of the agreement resulted in a further purging of his already diminishing network of friends—a network increasingly composed of sycophantic hangers-on—in addition to the elimination of a source of much-needed income.

I tried to help Marty, of course; but, particularly after my retirement, I was unable to give him as much support as he needed. And so, he spent one February in Georgia with no heat, and one July with no electricity: no lights, no refrigerator, no fan or air conditioner. I sometimes flew across country to take him to his doctors' appointments—at Grady Hospital in Atlanta where I had once worked—where security always hung around us because they could make no sense of this strange, extremely tall, long-haired white man exuding so much anger. His verbal abuse toward me was noted on more than one occasion by hospital staff who took him aside and called him out on it—something that only incensed him more.

Finally, I had no choice but to move my brother out to California, where, in his loneliness and his shock and his declining health and the loss of his house and his car and his dog and his friends, he just became a hater of everything. I tried to be sympathetic but so much of my energy was spent helping him obtain housing, SSDI benefits, and medications—all while troubleshooting crises—and, finally, the diagnosis from San Francisco General that my brother had long been suffering from multiple sclerosis. Sadly, it didn't get better for Marty out here in California: right in the midst of a nasty fight to prevent his apartment manager from evicting him (unlawfully) for being a smoker, Marty had a stroke that left him barely able to talk and no longer able to play his beloved guitar. All his efforts and anguish had seemingly resulted in no better prospects for the future. He became even more of a bitter, broken man.

When Marty's ancient computer failed, I gave him my old laptop, and when he discovered Facebook, he immediately began posting for someone to rescue him from his evil sister in California, and let him move in with them so he could live out whatever remaining time he had left in the land that he knew, that he felt comfortable in. In return, he would share part of his meager SSDI benefits for room and board. I watched in awe as he received serious offers from four different women. The stories of these selfless women and their attempts to take my brother in is another story in its own right; but the story here must include one woman, Debbie, who did it: who flew out to California three years ago, snatched Marty from the lonely liberal bowels of hell out here, and moved him into her home in south Georgia where, amazingly, they appear to be living—as The Turtles once sang, "so happy together." I've gotten to know Debbie over these last few years—she has graciously hosted me in her home twice—and she is a lovely, witty, well-educated woman who teaches sociology at Valdosta State University—and who once dated Marty briefly in the early 70s. While I was elated at my brother's good fortune, I remained dumbfounded as to why Debbie so willingly opened up her home and her heart to, essentially, Bartleby the Scrivener.

That is, until a stranger spoke only six words to me this past Friday morning while I was shopping at Trader Joe's. I was busy loading groceries into the back of my car when I caught sight of a man coming through the Trader Joe's parking lot behind me. Ordinarily, I doubt I'd have paid much attention, but as he neared me he seemed to slow down, at the same moment that I was feeling a don't-I-know-you flash. He stopped at the back of my car, giving me a chance to give him a good look, and I realized who he was, or might be. I moved to Alameda from Chicago in 1986. Almost from day one I often saw a man standing on a certain corner on Park Street, smoking a cigarette outside a gift shop. I walked past him, drove past him, jogged past him countless times. But I always noticed him. He seemed to own the corner, and I felt like some secret acknowledgment was in order, if that isn't an oxymoron. I can't say whether I ever actually spoke to him or not—most likely I said a friendly hello a time or two—without response I believe. I never saw him talking with anyone. He seemed to take no notice whatsoever of me; either that, or it was outright rejection: he wasn't friendly as most men were to me back then.

But he always struck me as an interesting character. I was often in the area—always in transit yet able to observe him through the years. Despite the adage that you can't judge a book by its cover, we do, in fact, "read" people all the time. People are like art or poetry: they are intrinsically what they are, but to each one of us, they are what they are *to us.* And we indulge ourselves all the time, fitting someone into our self-created metaphors of what love and life and relationships are, expanding a person in one direction, diminishing her in another. As so very much of our thinking is actually unconscious, strangers can literally become the creations of our dreams.

And so, even though I wasn't looking for a relationship and not necessarily with this stranger whose name I still don't know, it was not without a quickened step of awkwardness mixed with a dawdling step of longing that I would pass him by on foot. By car, he was an emotional Doppler in that some tiny thing in me would intensify as my car approached him—standing there, sometimes smoking, by the 51-Stop—then dissipate as I passed him by.

He stood there, straight and tall, with dark, thick, longish hair. He had magnificent forearms, and a strong physical presence. Something about him gave me the sense there might be a Harley parked nearby. His manner suggested to me both an appreciation of and a disdain for the ambience of Park Street, an environment in which I was but one tiny transient piece, perhaps only in the background and never in his focus. I always passed him feeling a little relief mixed with a little regret.

For twenty or thirty years now, this gentleman has been for me a bright spot on the urban landscape of Alameda. Almost imperceptibly, he has changed over the years, of course. Eventually, his deportment relaxed and I would see him leaning against the window of the gift shop or against the Bus Stop pole. Over time, he added a cane to his attire, although he still stood straight and tall. Then, for some months I thought that he had gone—but, no, there he was, sitting on the bench at the bus stop, apparently between smokes. For the past several years, I haven't been frequenting that area and so I haven't seen or really thought of him that much, if indeed he might still be there . . .

And so now, looking down at this gentleman—he was in a wheelchair—I pieced together all of the quick visual clips and snippets of him I'd gathered from many angles over many years, and I knew he was that same man.

"Well, hello!" I said warmly. "You're the man that I used to always see outside the gift shop on Park Street, aren't you?" He nodded. It was definitely his face, perhaps a little softer than I remembered, perhaps because I had never, until now, seen him smile. I plunked the cardboard wine box full of groceries in the car—I don't buy the paper bags at Trader Joe's when I forget my own bags, I just use their free cardboard boxes, they work perfectly and are better for my back—distracting myself with the groceries because I wasn't sure what else I could say to this man. I didn't know him, didn't know anything about him.

"Yeah, I always used to see you—always out there on that corner," I repeated. And then he said something to me, something I couldn't understand. There was animation in his eyes and a vibrancy to his lips and perhaps even a bit of a chirp in his voice that made me think he might be saying something a little cheeky. What was perfectly clear, however, was that this man had suffered a stroke that had affected his ability to speak.

"I'm sorry," I said. "I didn't quite catch that." He said the same thing again, and again, I caught none of it. "One more time?" I asked, leaning down and getting a little closer to him. I watched his face contort a little as he fell helpless to an impish grin that spread across his face and further impeded his efforts to form his words. How many times had I seen that same look in my brother's face. "I was looking for you!" he said.

I took in a deep breath and then laughed out loud. He's clever, I thought—like my brother, a wit that has an inexorable need to escape against any odds. As I finished laughing, I slammed the car hatch closed, pulled the keys out of my jeans pocket, then turned to him again. The man was positioned to roll on, but hadn't yet made his move to leave.

It was a lovely spring morning and so I asked him: "How are you feeling today?" He smiled and gestured for me to move in closer so I could better understand him. When I was just inches from his face, he whispered in my ear. "Horny," he said. Again, I let out a belly laugh and smiled at him, shaking my head and laughing. The man laughed too and seemed to take a moment to appreciate my appreciation of his mischievous wit. Then he wheeled past me on down the parking lot. I stood there a moment and watched him roll away, then got in my car and drove off.

My Family

Janet Brown

My family's history began in a small village in China. During the 1920s the Chinese people were suffering from famines, poverty, and turmoil created by fighting among warlords. My grandfather saw that immigration to the United States or "Golden Mountain," California, was the key to the family's survival. Somehow, he obtained passports for his family in the name of Lee. That is not our ancestral name. I believe it to be Chow or Choi, but this was never spoken of for fear of deportation. After a rough sea voyage, my father and grandparents were interned on Angel Island. My father Edward (Tong) Chow Lee was about thirteen years old at the time.

Following a long internment, they settled in Oakland Chinatown, where the family grew to five children including my uncles Warren and Joe and aunties Daisy and Mabel. My grandparents worked very hard. My grandfather was a handyman and my grandmother was a seamstress in a garment factory. By saving and borrowing funds through the Lee Family Association, they eventually owned five properties near what is now Laney College.

As a young man during World War II my father worked in the Kaiser shipyards. Following the war he found work at the fish canneries in Washington State, during which time he would send the bulk of his pay back home to help support his siblings.

My mother was an American by several generations, but one would never have known. Her grandfather had immigrated to the United States during the Gold Rush. She was born Mabel Hong in Courtland, California, where she enjoyed a normal childhood until the age of eight, when her mother decided to send her and her brother Tom to China, where they lived with an aunt and uncle who were childless. Her brother was sent to study with a scholar during the day, while my mother was expected to toil in the rice fields and perform duties as her aunt's "house slave." Life with her aunt and uncle was bleak, especially for an American-born girl. Work in the rice paddies was physically demanding, and at the end of a long day she was forced to sleep on a wooden pallet only after completing household chores and attending to her aunt. Mother never lost her spirit however, and was beaten frequently.

When China was faced with another famine, they were sent back to the US because the aunt and uncle couldn't afford two additional mouths to feed. Upon arrival they were kept on Angel Island, even though they were natural-born Americans. Settling in San Francisco, Mother eventually found work as a seamstress for Levi Strauss and working in the kitchen at several Chinese restaurants.

My mother and father's marriage was arranged. Dad was a very controlling person and Mom was very outspoken. It was not a match made in heaven. Despite this, they had four children, Allen, Lorna, Rhoda, and me, Moi Moi, or little sister. Although born in the United States, Mother did not retain her English. It was lost during her years toiling in China. Mother expressed an interest to relearn her native tongue, but being controlling, Father forbade it. He said all she needed to do was stay at home and raise the kids, so why was it necessary? Always headstrong, she taught herself English by watching TV, specifically daytime soap operas. Eventually my parents got a divorce, something unheard of at the time among Chinese families. My brother, Allen, was raised by my grandmother and we three girls by my father. I was five when my parents divorced. Ever controlling, my father forbade my mother to see us. When my own son turned five, my husband insisted we find her. At the age of twenty-nine, I was reunited with my mother after twenty-four years.

It was tough growing up without a mother during my formative years, but I had many aunts, uncles, and cousins.

When I turned eighteen I decided to pursue a nursing program at Laney College. There I met my husband, Thom Brown. He was twenty-nine and I was nineteen at the time. He claims it was love at first sight! We have been together since November 1969 and were married October 8, 1972. We had a hippie wedding in Jackson Park in Alameda. Not having a lot of friends in Alameda at the time, we posted signs, inviting the neighborhood to attend our "no hoopla" wedding. There was a band in the gazebo and a friend of my husband's arrived with a yellow hippie bus full of libations. The wedding is still spoken of to this day.

My husband and I had two children, Dr. Darren Brown and Kim Lee Dye. In 1976 we purchased our home in Alameda, near the old Del Monte cannery that later became a warehouse. At the time, it was constantly bustling with activity with trucks and trains pulling in and out at all hours. Del Monte has long since moved on, along with our children.

In retirement and with an empty nest, my husband and I discovered a love of teaching. We both taught through the Oakland Unified School District's Adult Education Program, and I taught in the Alameda School District also. I taught yoga at Mastick

Senior Center for many wonderful years. I still get together with "the ladies" from my yoga class every two months, to eat and chat at local restaurants.

My father passed away in 1996 and my mom in 1999. Two of my siblings, Allen and Rhoda, have also passed on, both on the same date but four years apart, each at the age of sixty-two. Rhoda, a runner and athlete who had never smoked a day in her life, died of lung cancer. My brother, tall, slim, and handsome, died of an undiagnosed heart problem. In 2011 our daughter bore us a grandson, Beckett Dye, so life goes on. Beckett, who is one-fourth Chinese, is considered fifth-generation Chinese American. He was born with light-brown hair and gray-blue eyes like my husband's. I look forward to telling him to one day about his rich heritage and all of those who came before him.

THE CHRISTMAS I'LL ALWAYS REMEMBER

Shirley S. (Lee) Daguman

Twelve days before Christmas our son was born. He was the family's first grandson. Christopher Jonathan (CJ) was born in the winter of 1980. It had been a frigid winter, plagued with heavy rain and wind. I was twenty-five years old, and Christopher was my first pregnancy. My pregnancy had been as dreary as the season, with the problems and fears that accompany any gestation that doesn't seem quite right. I had morning sickness, and would feel like throwing up when I smelled food cooking.

The news of discovering that the clan was expecting to add a name to the group was received with excitement. I began having my first contractions at 9:00 p.m. on Saturday, December 13, 1980. I called the hospital, and the nurse on duty knew by the tone of my voice that this was my first baby. She asked me to monitor the contractions since she knew I was overly excited. She told me that when the contractions were ten to fifteen minutes apart I should call the hospital again, and I would be admitted. Well, by 8:00 a.m. on Sunday morning, December 14, 1980, I felt the contractions again, and this time I knew it was time to go. My husband nervously drove me to Letterman Hospital in the Presidio in San Francisco. I went into labor at 10:00 a.m. that morning, for nearly seven hours. It felt like forever. External monitoring indicated fetal distress. I had a cesarean delivery, and my son was born at 4:50 p.m. that day. Christopher Jonathan was beautiful. He had delicate wispy features, satiny-smooth skin, and a tiny head covered lightly with fine brown hair.

Both of our families were always visiting us during our six-day stay in the hospital. The circumcision was performed Saturday morning and we left the hospital Sunday morning. The first two weeks my husband shared the excitement of caring and waking up in the middle of the night to feed Christopher. I would breast-feed him between bottle feedings. Oh, the joy of being a mother. The first two-week baby checkup went well. The doctor was to see Christopher two weeks later for his first immunization. But after our first visit I got an awful feeling in my stomach that Christopher wasn't feeling well. It my have just been my imagination, but I would get this ill feeling of fear about losing my baby. Christopher felt very warm that evening, so the next morning my mother drove CJ and me to Letterman Hospital. The intern doctor on duty said, "CJ is doing fine. Nothing to worry about." But that evening CJ had a temperature of 103, and I stayed up all night while my husband slept. The following morning January 24, 1981, we admitted our son into the hospital. The physician on duty took X-rays, blood, and spinal fluid, and the results were all negative. But CJ's temperature was still high, so they placed him under observation for three days.

Christopher Jonathan died two days later, on my birthday, January 26, 1981, of cardiac arrest with a viral infection. I did all my crying while sitting and watching my son's life slip away, and my grief at times seemed unbearable. My son had been the answer to so many of my prayers. It hadn't occurred to me that anything could happen to him, I had been so happy.

When I was expecting my baby, people were so kind and loving; they seemed truly happy for us. Nothing could have made his father and me happier. Every morning I woke up joyous with the thought of Christopher and what our lives would be like together, the three of us. Life itself had new meaning. I have never felt so close to God, and each day I would thank him for my baby, pray that I would have a happy healthy pregnancy, and give birth to a healthy baby. Carrying my son was the happiest and proudest time of my life. I loved his father, my husband, more than anything in the world, and the baby made our love seem so complete. When I lost Christopher, when he died, people felt our sadness; even strangers shared our grief. While sitting in the hospital after learning my son had left me, a nurse held me until his father could be with me, so I would not be alone.

People say I will never forget him. Christopher can never really be taken from me, as he is a part of me.

Now I look at life and the time we have on earth differently. I feel more love, compassion, and understanding for others. Every moment with his father is more precious. Life for me now is more valuable. I cherish each moment of my life, now that I realize how temporary our existence is on earth.

Pierrette Dick-Moore

The completion of the Golden Gate bridge in 1937 was the inspiration for my parents to relocate to Northern California from Santa Monica. My father's business was connected to the booming film industry in Hollywood; he and two partners owned a design studio that sold imported art, furniture, and other household decorations and furnishings. My parents were seeking a quieter locale to rear their growing family, three boys at that time. With the Golden Gate Bridge in place, Sonoma County was just an hour's drive north of San Francisco, but it was very tranquil due to its agricultural-based economy. There my parents bought several hundred acres of orchards planted with prune plums.

My father, Pierre Dick, had grown up in a French-speaking family in the Rhine River region. During his youth the area was under German occupation and no one was allowed to speak French. The local Alsatian dialect is based on German and he was educated in German schools, but he relearned French when he attended the University of Nancy after WWI, where he received a degree in fine arts.

Alsace-Lorraine became part of France again, and Pierre owed France his compulsory military service. He registered as a conscientious objector and joined the French Army Signal Corps, which maintained telegraph stations in outlying forts in remote areas of French territories. He was sent to the deserts of Morocco. He received a farewell gift of a Kodak Brownie camera, which he used to take pictures of the local sheiks and their wives, as well as of his companions in the fort. He developed the film himself with water from the wells where he was stationed. His fellow soldiers sent their families photos of themselves in their uniforms, executing their various duties. My father compiled three albums of small 2 x 4–inch photos, dated from the 1920s, that depict the local residents, villages, and animals. The photos surely are of archival value, but I have never located an interested party.

My father also learned to appreciate the handwoven rugs and finely made leather and brass items, sold in the local bazaars. His experience in Morocco, combined with his fine arts education and his experience growing up in a family that manufactured and sold furniture, easily led him to the business he established in Hollywood after his immigration to Southern California. He was amazed at the ease of life he discovered there and enjoyed daily swims in the Pacific Ocean. His younger brother Henry was already living in the area, having left France earlier, and had worked as a cowboy in Colorado before he found employment at the Golden State Dairy; Henry had always been interested in agriculture and animal husbandry. The brothers were the eldest in a family of six. Two younger brothers and a sister still lived in France. An older sibling had perished during the Spanish influenza pandemic while in boot camp, after being drafted by the German Army to fight in WWI. With Henry and Pierre's assistance, their younger brothers eventually immigrated to California as well. Their sister stayed in France with her husband and children.

Pierre encouraged Henry to join him and move his family north as well. Both brothers had found wives in Peoria, Illinois, where they had visited with families belonging to a congregation affiliated with their home church, the Apostolic Christians, a closely knit group of Anabaptists—they were among those called Huguenots, Protestants who had been emigrating from Europe for many years in order to escape persecution by the Catholic Church in France and Switzerland. Other Anabaptists are the Amish and Mennonites, considered the most liberal of their denomination.

Both of my parents' fathers had been lay ministers, conducting their services in German. Mother's family had immigrated to Illinois a century earlier but had maintained a connection with congregation members that still lived in Europe. My father kept his ability to speak German, French, and Alsatian until he died. He was a linguist by nature and had learned several other dialects in order to join the signal corps. My mother could understand both German and French, but as an American she spoke English, and her children were raised speaking English, and considered French-language classes to be a bothersome requirement while in school.

Henry came north to join his brother and managed the prune ranch. My father then bought a sheep ranch (later converted to a cattle ranch) in the foothills of the Alexander Valley, on the road to the geysers. This was long before PG&E had established the steam-energy production plant above Middletown, and the Old Geysers Road that was the route to our ranch was used mainly by tourists on their way to Mercuryville to observe the natural phenomenon.

My parents hired an architect in San Francisco to build a five-bedroom home on a ridge overlooking the Russian River Valley between Healdsburg and Geyserville. They were very happy when the project was completed in a mere ten weeks, as I arrived in August 1941, at Healdsburg Hospital. I now wonder how my father convinced my mother, Emily, to live with four young children in a rather inaccessible location they called the Ridge Ranch. Mother had trained as an RN while still living with her family in Illinois and was very interested in maintaining proper nutrition and hygiene. We grew our own vegetables and produced our own meat, milk, and eggs on the ranch, but nonetheless it was a thirty- to forty-minute drive each direction to purchase additional groceries, attend school, or receive medical care.

Our home was elevated a few feet above ground level and surrounded by porches in the style of a Japanese farmhouse. The area beneath the living spaces became infested with rattlesnakes, and I remember the mandate that no child was allowed off the porch unless accompanied by an adult. I can't recall the age limit that permitted free range but I am sure my older brothers' level of compliance was not high. It seems amazing that none of us ever were stricken by snakebite, but there are several tales of close calls within the family lore, as well as the story of a practical joke played on my father when a recently killed rattler was coiled in a lifelike manner and placed on the front porch steps to greet him as he returned from a trip.

The attack on Pearl Harbor four months after I was born convinced most local residents that another attack would soon follow in the Bay Area. I remember a small shack installed close to the house, near the clotheslines, that we called the observation post. It had maps on the walls and held a short-wave radio my mother used to report all aircraft sightings. My father located a cave on the back of the ranch, and he stored sleeping bags and enough food for two weeks there, should he need to evacuate our family of four small children, my mother, the au pair, and himself. Another residence on the property was occupied by the ranch foreman and his wife. Pierre's experience as a resident of disputed territory during WWI didn't lead him to expect aid or support from the outside if a military attack occurred in the region of his current home.

As gasoline rationing became a reality during the war years, it became unrealistic to drive my older brothers down to the valley to attend school. They were enrolled in a boarding school on the coast, north of Fort Ross, in a location now known as Salt Point. I think the youngest was only six years old when he joined the older two at the Stillwater Cove Boy's Ranch School. This solution was acceptable during the war, but afterward my mother wanted her boys at home, and by that time I also required an education, so my parents moved to Santa Rosa where we all could attend public schools. Kindergarten was my first experience with playmates other than my older brothers, and I clearly remember my first best friend, who lived across the street. We spent many happy hours coloring together while listening to the radio. Her father was still away in the army when we met, but after his return he found work with J. C. Penney and was soon transferred to Fresno. It was heartbreaking to lose her company.

Santa Rosa was the county seat and thus always a bigger town than Healdsburg, but during my school years it was still a small town with no industry. My father invested in the only decent restaurant in town, called the Topaz Room. It had been established by a wealthy Sonoma County lumberman who had traveled widely in Europe, and his wife had amassed a valuable collection of fine glassware, which my father highly appreciated due to his heritage.

During my elementary school years my family traveled frequently to my mother's hometown in Illinois to visit her family, which included many aunts, uncles, and cousins. In 1951 we also went to Europe because the relatives there who had survived WWII were anxious to meet their American cousins. My father's parents had not survived the war years due to poor health, and my maternal grandparents were deceased before I was born. This made the visits with aunts, uncles, and cousins extremely precious.

I still have very clear memories of the voyage across the Atlantic on the SS *Liberté,* and the following six weeks of travel in France, Switzerland (my paternal grandmother's homeland), and even to Morocco, where my father had served in the army.

While in Morocco we were invited into the native quarters as guests of the large family of a young man who was currently employed at the Topaz Room back in Santa Rosa. The United States was considered to be Utopia by Moroccans, and while we were in Marrakech my father befriended another young man, who was working as a busboy in the restaurant of the hotel where we were staying. My father had learned to converse in Arabic during his army assignment, and visited with him. This lad, of course, wanted to emigrate as well, so my father assisted him to come to Santa Rosa and work in the Topaz Room. I remember that the young man later moved to Las Vegas and eventually became the captain of the dining room at the Sands Hotel. He had married a woman from home and they raised a family together until he died in a car accident. He had stayed in touch with my family, and never ceased to show his appreciation for the opportunity we gave him to become as US citizen.

I lived in Santa Rosa until my college years. I spent my last three years in high school at the Katherine Branson boarding school in Ross because the local high school was very crowded. The GI Bill created a housing boom, and there was plenty of room to build in Sonoma County. My father participated by developing several subdivisions, including some of the first homes in Rohnert Park.

My three older brothers went off to college, and I was also away at Katherine Branson. Now the large family home that had been built outside Santa Rosa was more than my parents wanted to maintain, so they put it on the market and went back to live on the Ridge Ranch on the old road to the geysers. They rented the home they had built there in 1941 from the current owner, who had moved from the East Coast and then married into the Pedroncelli family, which grew grapes and produced wines. During her tenure a swimming pool had been installed. My father relished it, recalling the joy of his daily swims in the ocean while in Southern California. We had also had a pool at our home in Santa Rosa, and he had loved an evening swim. The summer temperatures at the ranch were much higher because the heat from the valley floor would rise, and the ranch was usually above the fog layer. Neither of these pools was heated, and we all thought it a great luxury when the water temperature reached into the 70s. My father loved the Ridge Ranch and had yearned to return ever since the move to Santa Rosa after the war. When he died we scattered his cremains there.

My cousins, whose father, Henry, had moved them north on my father's advice, continue to live in Sonoma County. Cousin Ron never left the prune ranch. He attended college at Davis in the early sixties and recommended to his father that they replace some of the prune orchards with grapes. The property originally purchased by my parents before I was born now produces some very fine grapes and is known as Belle Terre Vineyard. Ron's sister Jeanette lives adjacent to the vineyards as well. There had always been a few wineries in Sonoma County, and I remember visiting the Beringer sisters in their lovely big home in Sonoma. They were Swiss, as was my father's mother, and we would at times stop by and have tea with them. It is even possible that they also were members of the Apostolic faith, as those ties ran very deep. My father's maternal aunt in Switzerland married into the Sutter family, whose members included John Sutter, the pioneer at whose California mill gold was discovered in 1848.

While in college at the University of Colorado I got married, and I didn't return as a resident of Sonoma County until twenty years later. I was lucky enough to live in Tiburon for about two years when my children were small, but my husband's career required moving a few times, once for a job in New Jersey. I had never intended to live on the East Coast, but since I had managed to survive a few years in the Midwest, I was adaptable enough to make it through a couple of winters in the East before we moved to Denver, my husband's hometown.

After a divorce and a second marriage I was delighted to return to the Bay Area in 1980. My second husband's occupation in the oil business took him to the San Francisco financial district. He commuted from Santa Rosa, so I could now live near my parents, who had once again moved away from the Ridge Ranch in order to enjoy the amenities offered by living in Santa Rosa. Alas, my husband's job then required a move to Houston. I could hardly believe I was once again leaving what I considered to be the only part of the world where I could enjoy living. Furthermore, my parent's fiftieth wedding anniversary and my older stepdaughter's wedding were both scheduled to take place on the porch of the home we had just built looking over the Rincon Valley. But it was not meant to be. Each event found another venue, and I reluctantly became a resident of the Gulf Coast, where we experienced both tornadoes and a hurricane in our first year of residence.

After three years there, we returned to my beloved California. Fortunately, I was living in Alameda during the final years of my parents' lives, and I visited them as often as my job at the Kaiser Center in Oakland allowed. Destiny didn't intend for me to stay in the Bay Area, however, and my husband and I tried to enjoy our retirement on the coast of Oregon. It soon became clear that that was not where we belonged, and it seemed like a fine time to buy an RV and look for the right place. After three wonderful summers spent touring British Columbia we decided to explore the

Southwest. It was such a peaceful area that we easily chose to build a home in the desert, where we lived very quietly until his death in 2005. I stayed on for several years in the small town just twenty-five miles north of the Mexican border, returning to California in 2010.

During those earlier years, as I migrated across the country, I enjoyed rearing my two daughters and a developing relationship with two stepdaughters of the same age. I often worked, first as a volunteer, then as a business owner, and finally as a travel agent. In New Mexico I trained as a child advocate supervised by the courts, and volunteered in a program called CASA that monitored children in the foster care system. After my husband's death, my CASA work became a part-time job, and I recruited and trained other volunteers as well. This work gave my life great meaning while I learned to navigate widowhood. I had been with CASA for six years when my daughter asked me to return to the Bay Area to help her. She was eager to become an educational therapist and required a master's in education from Holy Names to launch that career.

When my husband was alive, we once drove to Point Lobos, where we had decided to marry during a visit in 1977, and we talked about where each of us would choose to go if we found ourselves alone. I always knew in my heart that I would return to the Bay Area. Once again I am back in Alameda, enjoying time with my daughter's family, watching my grandsons mature, and finding enrichment through the many classes and events at the Mastick Center.

Fathers Were Rationed Too

Karren Lutz Elsbernd

Sugar was rationed, butter was rationed, and fathers were rationed too. And so my father missed my first words, my first steps. Yet in the first year of my life, when he appeared on furlough from preparing for war, home just so briefly, I stood straight and tall upon his palm. He told that story, remembering my two small feet, steady on his one outstretched strong hand. My father was proud of me.

I stop playing and run to the curb shouting something like, *I can see them, the cars are coming!* The parade is once again coming just for us, the kids on Keokuk Street. I live here on the crest of this hill in a small California town, and I balance my feet on the curb to wait and watch. Next to the gnarled trunk of the pepper tree that grows at the dead center on the top of this little hill, I can see downhill in both directions. *They're coming!* The first car in our parade is always the same, long and black with no windows. Sometimes just a few cars follow and other times, many passed us. The parade is different each time but the people inside all wear the same grim faces. They do not smile at us, and neither do my friends or I raise our hands to wave at them. We just stand there staring, the heels of our shoes all lined up on the curb, our toes hanging over the edge.

Did our parents ever explain why those cars always took our street, up over our hill, to drive down to the cemetery at the city limits below? Would we have understood the word *funeral* then? I imagine it was one of many explanations omitted by my parents during my early life. Silence on certain subjects was not uncommon. Staying close to home, we were all innocently present when our parade arrived. With the two adjoining driveways alongside our yard, my house was an ideal place for the neighborhood to play under the supervision of my protective mother. I often stood next to the twisted trunk of the pepper tree, where I once saw a minute hummingbird's nest protected in its weeping branches.

They're here! In my memory I still see us balancing on the curb, waiting. We were plentiful, ranging in age from those of us born as our fathers had gone to war to those born after they returned. I was in the first category; my sister would be in the latter. All very young, as I was only five when we moved away from this house. I don't remember what games we would have been playing when the parade call came. Yet I can see us lined up, no one venturing further than that curb, the demarcation line before the forbidden street. Solemn, silent, we stood there and watched, leaving behind for that brief moment the shouting, laughing and playful quarreling. Somehow we understood the somber occasion, the black hearse, the faces of the mourners, without knowing the words. My sister and I would be spared death in that war; we did not lose our father, uncles, or cousins. It was never really *our* parade. Each time a funeral came, it passed us quietly, and we had no need to follow it to the end of the street.

Between the tall father in his uniform and the mother in her plaid dress a very young girl stands holding the hands of both, wearing her V for Victory pin. Another family portrait before the father is gone again. A single moment in my life caught in black and white, to be saved in the photograph album. Today my father and mother are gone, and being too young to remember that day, I now regret never being told the story of my first years. My story began before I was born, when an attack shocked their world and my tall soon-to-be father was drafted into that war. I am conceived just before he, a Kansan, leaves to train for combat in the South Pacific. She, an Idahoan, is left behind in this small California town, in the house on the top of the hill, where I would be born and live my first two and half years until my father is returned home whole and safe. I imagine my parents put the trials of the war years behind them as quickly as possible. Those years of separation became a subject never spoken about for the remainder of their lifetimes. And along with their silence, those first years of my life were put aside too.

Other evidence was put away too, including my father's army dog tags and my own ration card (Occupation: baby). From all those objects put aside and saved, and safe now with me, I often try to piece together the story of that little girl. There with the other items is the fuzzy little pin, still with its small safety pin clasp, worn in so many photographs. A circle of red and white yarn with a white V stitched in its blue center, handmade just for me, to be worn when I did my patriotic part to end that war and make sure my father came home to me. We soon outgrew the small house at the top of the hill with the addition of a father, and a sister on the way. A new family story was beginning.

I was never brave enough to break the taboo of silence about that time, and now no one is left to tell me the stories of my first years. Only the photographs have been saved, including the one that confirms my brave hand-held feat. My life changed, and I became one of many smiling kids on the top of the hill who gathered on the lawn to have their picture taken. I became a big sister. In a photograph my mother took of us, my father, no longer in uniform, holds a new baby in his arms. I stand next to them, a young shy girl growing taller and taller.

A Day at the Beach

Isabella Gussoni Fahrney

In the summer of 1965 we moved from Castro Valley to San Francisco, where I quickly discovered that the weather rarely looked promising. One morning I saw that a ray of sun was visible through the fog, and I decided to take the children—Barbara, four, and David, two and half—and our German shepherd, Dimmi, to the beach. When we arrived at Ocean Beach the wind was blowing so hard and the sand swirling so powerfully that I could not even open the door of the car. I didn't give up. Sitting in the car I examined a local map and found Alameda, which looked like it had a beach. I had never been to Alameda before but I assumed that it would be warmer there because it was close to Oakland, where I knew summer existed.

We already had a lunch packed, so I put the top down on the 1960 Cadillac and drove us off on this new adventure. We reached Alameda by the Webster Street tube, and I remember my first impression of the island: sailors and bars everywhere. We reached Otis Drive, where plots of land had been partitioned but nothing had been built yet (there was no South Shore shopping center). I found the beautiful deserted beach along Shoreline Drive. The sun was out and the water was calm and sparkly. We played and ate lunch. When it was time to leave, because it was warm and we were going straight home, I had the idea of driving in my bathing suit.

We lived in a quiet residential area in the Haight-Ashbury district, and I did not expect to see anybody on our way.

I drove us across the Bay Bridge, and as we approached the Fell Street exit, I suddenly saw a small Falcon spinning around against the traffic in front of us. In no time it hit my car. The Falcon was practically demolished, the Cadillac seemed unharmed. The other driver and all of us were fine.

As we waited for the police I decided I should check the damage to the Cadillac, and so I found myself, at the height of afternoon commuter traffic, standing in a yellow polka-dot bathing suit next to a flashy black-and-red Cadillac with the top down and two little children and a German shepherd bouncing around in the backseat. Soon the "happy honking" started as I turned into entertainment for a dull commute. The police arrived but had a more urgent call, so they told us to exchange information and contact our insurance agencies.

I learned two lessons that day. The first was that people sometimes lie. The other driver told his insurance company that I had hit him, forgetting that we had been on a one-way freeway and he had come against the traffic. I gave my agent a diagram of the accident, and the man's claim was rejected. The damage to the Cadillac was a barely noticeable dent that cost sixty dollars to fix. The second lesson was: never drive anywhere unless properly dressed, no matter what.

The Great Depression, or My First Course in Economics

Sally Faulhaber

The first change in my life resulting from the Great Depression was our move from Berkeley to Iowa in October of 1934, when I was five years old.

It had been about a year since we had moved from North Oakland to Berkeley, to a house on Virginia Street close to Whittier School. I was lonely and bored for some time after the move. I missed my friends from Dover Street, especially Bill Manly, one of the three friends Mom allowed me to invite to my fourth birthday.

After a few months, things on Virginia Street got better. There were a lot of activities going on at the schoolyard (something to do with the Long Beach earthquake and the concern it raised about the safety of school buildings). I spent a good deal of time there in the dances Mom directed, where we never quite got the chain dance to work, and carving soap and learning to travel on the traveling rings. On our block a bunch of us sometimes got on the flat roof of a garage and danced and talked about ghosts, one of which lived in my closet. We dared to go part way up the stairs of the haunted house around the corner until a woman in the next house threatened to call the police on us. That really scared me. I was scared again when I climbed a big pine tree next to the church across the street and a woman looked at me from the second floor of the church, the level I was on, and said she would call the cops. We climbed on the roof of our house too, my brother, John, and I and some of his friends. I'm sure Mom didn't know. Once we sat on the roof over the back door and discussed making a parachute from a sheet, but we weren't sure it would work. But there were tamer things: We played checkers and argued over whether you could double king a piece, and Mom started giving me piano lessons. The front porch was a boat and I learned to tie knots. We played hide-and-seek and I learned to count to one hundred by fives.

Dad had gotten a new job, his dream job, with a small company called McCorkle Controls. He was on very cordial terms with Mr. McCorkle, and had even been made a vice president of the company. But sometime in 1934, the company ran out of money and couldn't pay him. I later learned that our family accumulated considerable debt, a condition echoed seventy years later in the 2008 recession.

My mother's mother, Grandma Lamb, had some property in Iowa, or at least control of it. Grandpa Frank Lamb had inherited several houses and farms from his father, who died in 1929, but Frank was mentally incapacitated with what was then called premature senility. Grandma offered us one of her houses in Spencer. Both of my parents were from Iowa, and Dad had connections in Spencer from his work there when he was in high school. The Depression was hitting California hard. So my parents decided to move back to Spencer.

We traveled to Iowa on a bus. I don't remember much, except being told not to go to the water cooler so often. The cups were little white paper cones. I must have slept through a good deal of the trip, which might explain why, for several years afterward, I thought the ocean was just west of the Rockies.

Mother, John, and I lived at first with Grandma and Grandpa Lamb in another of Grandma's holdings, a small resort in Arnold's Park, and Dad rented a room in Spencer. Grandma had agreed to let us have a house in Spencer, a house Mom referred to as her Grandpa and Aunt Mary's, but Grandma had leased the place until March, so it wasn't available until then.

Arnold's Park was a small resort community on East Okoboji Lake. The property had a string of resort cabins named for presidents, but they were all closed for the winter. The house was a sort of hotel with lots of little rooms. I had a second-floor room to myself for sleeping, and John did also. Mom had a bigger room at the end of the floor, with windows overlooking the lake, and Dad stayed with her on weekends. All those rooms were cold. The only heat upstairs was in the bathroom, so we dressed in there.

For me those five months in Arnold's Park were boring. I only had one playmate, Jane Hazzard, who lived across the road. She was pretty and nice, but had no spirit. I gathered from things half spoken that her father had some kind of problem, maybe drinking. Her grandfather lived at the top of the hill. He was a blacksmith, and one of the more interesting things I did was watch him sharpening tools on a wheel and occasionally heating some piece of metal in a forge until it glowed red. He and his wife seemed very old. She had no teeth. I sometimes sat with them in their kitchen, which was dark and had a peculiar smell, some combination of tobacco and stale grease. I wanted to go to first grade, but Mom wouldn't let me, and there was no kindergarten there. The only thing I remember being taught was how to tie a bow. Mom got a red ribbon and showed me how to tie it around part of a chair.

Cold was a new experience. One afternoon I played in the goldfish pond until my hands hurt. When they started to warm up they hurt even more for several minutes. As the winter progressed this became a familiar sensation. We called it chilblains. One morning I looked out at the lake and was amazed to see someone walking on the water. I didn't understand, but soon I was allowed to walk on it too, when Mom thought the ice was thick enough.

There were good hours too, when Mom took me walking along the shore, and one magic morning when all the trees were coated with hoarfrost, and Mom bundled me and John and Jane in warm clothes, and we walked across Gar Lake and slid down the slopes in the snow.

But for the most part it was a time of stress. Dad was away most of the week. Grandma was busy dealing with Frank, who mostly sat in a chair and sometimes babbled unintelligibly. I was confined by the cold and much of the time had nothing to do.

In March we moved into the house in Spencer, and I entered kindergarten in the North School. I didn't know any of the kids and they all knew each other. My partner in dancing was Harvey, who was tall and rather stupid and had black hair and black teeth. John got the mumps and a little later I got them. I was only sick for one day but had to stay out of school for a week.

That spring Mom and Dad planted a huge garden. They spaded the deep, black soil and stretched strings from sticks to make straight lines and plant vegetables in straight rows. The following summer Mom canned tomatoes and corn relish. Mom papered and painted the walls and refinished a second-hand table for the dining room. Dad built a breakfast nook in the kitchen and a corner cupboard in the dining room.

It must have been the next winter that was so cold our car stayed in the garage for months. Several times Dad crawled into a basement space along the edge of the house, with a torch to thaw the freezing pipes. I remember standing in front of the heat register in the dining room to get warm. We weren't heating the living room or anything upstairs except the bathroom, so that was where we dressed.

The basement had a big old coal-burning furnace, a pale-gray monster with many arms. I watched Dad down there working on another of his inventions, a device to convert a coal-burning furnace to one that burned oil. He used this to get a job with Perfection Stove Company, but the job he got was not in engineering as he had hoped, but in sales. He became a traveling salesman, covering Iowa and Minnesota, selling furnaces to dealers. So again he was gone for the weekdays and home only on weekends. That was his job for the next five years.

Meanwhile, I was in first grade, still shy and somewhat lost in the social sphere. We were still poor. The rug in the living room was so threadbare that I was allowed to roller-skate on it. I was out of school for several weeks in the fall with impetigo, a skin infection, which was especially difficult to treat with the medicines of the day, and again in the winter with tonsillitis, but both times I was promoted out of the intermediate reading group to the fast one within a week of my return.

In the winter of 1936–37 we got a new oriental rug and a davenport and pair of end tables for the living room from Montgomery Ward. Grandpa Lamb died and my sister Margaret was born. A girl named Annette came to my second grade class and within a day or two we had discovered we had much in common and became such good friends that we could finish each other's sentences. She was the only really close friend I ever had. At the end of her street there were two houses left unfinished after the Crash, and we liked to walk along the edges of the foundations and look down into the basements.

Mom's inheritance from her father's estate included the house we were living in and the acreage south and west of it. The western part was planted in corn, but the part to the south, about three lots wide, was an old alfalfa field left fallow. The resort on East Okoboji went to my Aunt Frances, and a cabin on the lagoon near West Okoboji Lake to my Aunt Elinor. Every summer Sunday we went to the lakes in the company car, always a Chevrolet, at first to the resort and later to the cabin.

With the newly acquired property and a steady job, my parents decided to build a new house, into which we moved in the late summer of 1938.

The financial crisis was past, Dad was selling lots of furnaces, Mom had arranged for a poor family from the other end of town to sharecrop most of the garden, and we could buy some clothes from a place other than Montgomery Ward. But Mom was still frugal. Mom missed her artsy friends in Berkeley, and Dad missed the philosophical and political conversation of the Unitarians they knew there. We survived the Depression without terrible scars, with family help and an enterprising spirit. But it was a different life.

My Teenage Years in Holland

Nell Fliehmann

In 1953, when I was thirty years old, I immigrated to the United States. I was a Dutch citizen and five years later became an American citizen. I had spent my youth in Indonesia and my teenage years in Holland. I still have many fond memories of my early years.

In 1932, when my parents moved our family back to Holland after living in Indonesia for many years, we lived temporarily in a furnished old stately canal home in the historic city of Delft, known for its University of Technology, its old City Hall, the New and Old Churches, and for Delft blue porcelain. My oldest brother, Piet, was already living there, having arrived six months earlier to attend the university.

Because of the Great Depression my father had been pensioned off at only forty-five years of age. He had four children, two girls in grammar school, one boy in high school, and another boy in university. Since 1929 the entire world had been in the grip of the depression. We heard of long breadlines in New York. Many people were unemployed, and in general the standard of living was not very high, so people lived modest lives. My mother squeezed every guilder and taught us to be frugal by example. That trait has stayed with me for the rest of my life.

My other brother, Fred, and my sister, Truus, and I were immediately enrolled in the local schools. Every day while walking home from school, I passed the unemployment office. There were always men loitering about, standing against the wall, sitting on the sidewalks, and one day a man was lying flat out in the street. He looked lifeless. I was quite upset and hurried home.

After a few months my parents started looking around for a house where Piet could join us and all six of us 'could once again live together. They found a house in Rijswijk, a suburb of the Hague, and a short distance from the university where Piet was a student. Since my father was receiving a small pension he could only afford a modest rental home. The house did not even have a bathroom, and only two of the three small bedrooms had a washbasin. To take a bath I had to walk.to the local bathhouse in town, where I paid a fee for which I received a small bar of soap and a towel. I hated going there because I had trouble adjusting the hot and cold faucets and often scalded myself with piping-hot water.

Truus and I were in grammar school. We had never expected that we would not be accepted by the other students because we came from Indonesia. Truus made a friend, but when the girl invited her to stop by her home she said, "Please do not ring the front door bell. Walk around and come to the rear of the house." This was so that other kids would not find out about her visits. I was not greatly bothered by not being accepted. But obviously my teacher noticed because one day she called me over and told me that there would be a new student of my age from Indonesia and she felt we could be friends. Miep arrived, a chubby dark-haired girl. Indeed we became instant friends, well beyond grammar school.

My mother no longer had paid domestic help at home. Her two daughters had to help with household chores, whereas Piet and Fred were never asked to do anything. That is the way my mother was raised and that is how she raised us. In those days in Holland, boys usually went on to higher education and girls were expected to marry a man with a good education, become a mother, and be a housewife.

My father could not find a job. Many men were unemployed and so was he. He took care of the garden and did the shopping. He liked to go fishing, and one day he asked me to join him. It sounded exciting, but the fish were not biting and pretty soon I was bored sitting in a small rowboat, having little success catching anything.

When Fred graduated from high school, my mother gave a party for him. The party was well attended by his friends, and afterward my sister and I, who had not been invited to the party, had to wash the dirty dishes. While Truus was busy sorting things out, I was walking up and down the hall on my wooden stilts. I walked on them up to her, standing at the sink, and I, a brat of ten, challenged her. "Give me a hard push and I will show you that I will not fall off these stilts." So she did. What a mistake, to do this right at the kitchen counter. She gave me a forceful whack and I fell over onto the counter. Glasses, plates, cups, and saucers came crashing down. At least we did not have to wash them, but we both spent a lot of time picking up the shattered dishes. Truus told my mother that it had been my idea and my mother was pretty upset with me.

Another time our family of six was having dinner. I was around eleven, and my brother Piet was asserting his seniority among us siblings. He and I got into a heated argument and I ended the argument by throwing a knife at him (making sure to miss him). Immediately a fork zoomed by my head (he also made sure to miss me): the prongs of the fork became embedded in the piano behind me, and it slightly disfigured the face of the piano. Again my mother was not very happy with me.

We lived in Rijswijk for six years. Eventually both of my brothers graduated, left the house, and moved to Amsterdam. I finished high school. Now my parents decided to find a more comfortable house with a bathroom. They found a nice house to rent in the town of Wassenaar, then and now an affluent town and a suburb of The Hague. The modest homes are downtown, which is where we moved. The old queen of Holland had an estate somewhere in the woods there, and the present royal family lived in Wassenaar for a while.

After we moved to Wassenaar, my brothers would come home for the holidays like Christmas and New Year's Eve. I have wonderful memories of our New Year's Eve celebrations. We would play cards and drink mulled wine. Fred would usually find something he could tease me about. My mother made traditional foods such as fried-apple beignets: the apples were cored, sliced into thick slices, rolled in a batter, and then deep-fried and dusted with sugar powder.

Another traditional dish was a cold dish, like a potato salad, and contained pickled marinated beets, chopped boiled potatoes, small cubes of tender beef, and chopped gherkins. All of these ingredients were mixed together and then formed into an oval mound and spread with mayonnaise, and decorated with slices of tomato and hardboiled eggs. At midnight we would listen to the radio broadcast about all the important happenings of the past year, while enjoying mulled wine, eggnog, or a homemade drink of cherries and brandy.

Christmas in Holland is a religious holiday, without gift giving. My mother, with the help of Truus, would prepare a festive Christmas meal. Usually we had rabbit as the main course, and a colorful floral centerpiece with candles graced the dining table. My mother would go to church. I recall one Christmas when she said to me, "There is a Christmas service in church, and all young people who attend will receive a box of candy." Needless to say, I attended that service. I remember that we sat in the rear of the church, and at the end of the service some parishioners came around handing out boxes of *Haagse hopjes,* a well-known hard-coffee candy in Holland. By the time they came to us they had run out, and they apologized to us. It was a disappointment for me, but let's face it, I had attended church for the wrong reason.

Gift giving was on December 5. The day was simply called Sinterklaas (Saint Nicholas). When I was young I loved that day. We celebrated by exchanging small gifts. Some traditional sweets were chocolate letters and marzipan. It was a custom to include a rhyme with our gifts. In the rhyme we would poke fun at one another's shortcomings. Our parents were not included in this game. Since it was all in the family, no one took offense.

Even though Fred was older by now, he had not changed much. With my allowance I bought my first ring and was happy to wear it. When Fred saw the ring he said, "Even though a monkey wears a beautiful ring, it is and remains an ugly thing."

In the summer of 1939, Truus and I and a small group of friends went on a bicycling trip and stayed overnight in youth hostels. We bicycled the width of Holland, and then continued south into Belgium. At that time there were rumors all along the way, confirmed by the newspapers, about Hitler's increasing aggressiveness. Dark clouds began to gather. When we arrived back home the news was not very encouraging about the events happening in Germany.

On May 10, 1940, World War II broke out. Norway, Denmark, Holland, Belgium, parts of France, and other countries became occupied by the German army. Soon our lives changed drastically, and much of the world became embroiled in this conflict. For me education and dating were interrupted, and we had to cope with severe food shortages. Soon finding clothing and shoes became a matter of exchange, barter, or doing without, since these items were no longer available in the stores. We lived under enormous stress and in constant fear of bombing from fighter planes coming from both England and Germany.

In western Holland, where we lived, the war ended on May 5, 1945. I had been seventeen years old when the war started and was twenty-two when hostilities ended. I continued to live in Holland for a little more than half a year and then left the country, returning only for occasional visits to my family. I eventually immigrated to the United States where, except for a period of twelve years, I have always lived in the San Francisco Bay Area. At ninety-four years of age I now look back on a long life filled with mostly good memories.

LIFE AT LINCOLN PARK

Catherine Folsom

I don't remember the first time I was taken to Alameda's Lincoln Park on High Street. I'm sure it was at a very early age because we lived on Santa Clara Avenue until I was in second grade. The images of Lincoln Park that come to mind are of a giant green iron fence with two wide entrances that seemed to reach almost to the clouds. The ancient, large trees that grew in the grassy area cast shade across the walking paths that led to the playground.

My mother would shop for groceries, meat, and drugstore needs at three little markets that lined High Street at Santa Clara Avenue. She would lift my two brothers and me into a double baby buggy that rocked from side to side as she pushed us to the store from our small white stucco house. Before shopping for groceries and other necessities we would be allowed to visit the park for some playtime, but only if we had behaved ourselves that morning.

I always felt we never got to spend enough time at Lincoln Park. After what seemed an endless stroll on the winding pathway to the swings, slide, and swinging bars, we would always run to the swings first. The activity of swinging brought happiness and contentment to me. Today, the swings are in the same location they were seventy years ago. However, hanging and swinging on the bars in the other part of the playground caused me fear and anxiety because eventually I'd have to let go and fall to the ground, which meant a hard landing for my tender feet.

There was one mysterious aspect to the park that puzzled me. There were two or three little houses on the grounds. At least they looked like houses to me. They appeared to be dark, with a feeling of loneliness emanating from the old stones and wood they were made of. Looking in the windows was useless; all you could see was solid grayness due to the dirty panes. Years later I found out the buildings were merely storage sheds for rakes, brooms, and other tools used to keep the gardens well tended.

My family had to move when I was in second grade. My father found a house only one block from my wonderful Lincoln Park, and I was now allowed to go to this favorite place alone. In those days there were park directors, who delighted us with team games, art activities, music, and companionship as well playground supervision for the safety of the children.

The years rolled by, and I found other places that appealed to me, like the Alameda Theater with its Saturday matinees that included a newsreel, cartoon, and double feature. What more could I ask? But Lincoln Park continued to be a place for young children to enjoy the adventures and fun I had enjoyed as a child.

I remained in Alameda, and when I married and began raising three boys, Lincoln Park again became the place to go. My husband and I enjoyed watching our little ones playing on the same slide and swings, and enjoying picnics and the activities offered there.

After several more years, we were able to introduce our grandchildren, Keona and Matthew, to this special place. I remember taking them the first time and recalling the long walk into the park I used to take with my own brothers.

The Bench

Noel Folsom

When I attended Haight Grammar School in Alameda in the mid-1940s, it was a beautiful white two-story building of classic design. The building itself was in the shape of the letter H. Classes were in the parallel wings of the building, the lower grades on the first floor and the upper grades on the second. The basement was divided in half, and on one side contained the boys' shop in the front of the building, and then as you worked your way back, there was the boys' gym and at the far end the boys' bicycle room. The same configuration existed on the opposite side, the girls' half. The cross section connecting these two wings contained a large auditorium with an upstairs balcony.

Entering the building from the broad front stairs, you climbed another set of stairs once inside. To the right as you entered was the school nurse's office and a smaller room where children who were sick enough to go home could wait for their parents to pick them up. The office to one's left as you entered was the secretary's office and behind that was the office of the principal; to the kids it seemed like the inner sanctum.

Directly across from the office's entrance was a large ornate wooden bench attached to the wall. A similar bench faced the nurse's office. It was bad enough to be seen sitting on the bench opposite the nurse's office, but it was the ultimate shame to be seen sitting in front of the principal's office. Everyone passing would look at you with either disdain or with a smile, because they knew that you had committed some serious misdemeanor and that you would sit there for all the world to see for the next hour or two.

My initiation to the bench happened about three months after I began my fifth grade classes, after transferring to Haight from Sadler School, a kindergarten through fourth grade school. I was in the middle of the only fight of my school career and was caught in the act of trading punches with another boy by the teacher on yard duty. The other boy and I were marched up to the principal's office and told to sit on the bench until the principal had time to see us.

The boy I got in the fight with was shorter than I was, but then I was always skinny, the tallest or second tallest boy in all my classes. He had a reputation, unbeknownst to me, of being a tough guy. I didn't know that since we had only traded a punch or two before the teacher intervened.

At first we didn't speak to each other. After a while, however, we started chatting out of sheer boredom. Still, the time dragged slowly and it was about an hour and a half before the secretary summoned us to the principal's office. By this time we were very nervous because we had heard stories of the principal spanking those who caused serious trouble, or calling their parents, a significant threat in those days because you knew if the punishment at school was bad, it would be even worse when you got home or, heaven forbid, your mother was called in to pick you up and you were seen by your peers.

Once we got into the principal's office, he had us sit down and tell him why we were there. He was almost kindly, after our imaginations had run wild thinking of all the possible things he could do to us. After we gave our respective sides of the story, he pondered what to do. After some thought—which added to the tension—he decided we should go down to the boys' gym the next morning and fight it out in the boxing ring. Neither the other boy nor I now thought this was a good idea as we had become somewhat friendly during our long session on the bench, but since the solution did not include a note or a call to our parents, we readily agreed to it.

The next morning we met in the boys' gym, took off our shirts, leaving on our undershirts, and climbed into the ring. The principal then presented each of us the largest pair of boxing gloves I had ever seen. They were huge, well padded, and heavy! Once the gloves were laced and checked by the principal, he told us to go to it and fight. Neither one of us had the heart, but we had no choice with the principal looking on and urging us to punch one another.

I don't know how we did it, but we both figured out independently that it would be best to slug it out. We certainly did, and when either one of us slowed down because of fatigue, the principal urged us to keep swinging. The gloved blows were nothing compared to the pain in the arms from the constant act of punching. We were both breathing pretty hard and reeling from the weight of the gloves when we were finally told to stop, take the gloves off, and shake hands. This we did, with pleasure. As we handed the gloves to the principal, he admonished us never to fight again on school grounds.

The final embarrassment was coming into the classroom late, after our boxing match. The teacher told us to take our seats quietly and open our textbooks to the page of the lesson in progress. Neither one of us said a word about our experience to our classmates, we just let the issue die.

The benefit of having a wise principal was that the other boy and became pretty good friends and neither one of us was in a fight at the school again.

ISLANDS AND CANYONS

Robert Frank

I was born long ago in the briar patch that is Manhattan, in a hospital that once stood at 531 East 86th Street, only one block away from the mayor's digs, Gracie Mansion. I was the first of two children born to my mom and dad, a loving couple who weathered many storms during the course of their fifty-five-year marriage.

My dad was a WWII vet. He met my mom at a roller skating rink in the Bronx and started dating her before he went overseas. He was in Bastogne, Belgium, at the Battle of the Bulge, Germany's last big offensive. Mom told me she became ill when she saw the news about that battle. Germans massacred Americans they captured there instead of taking them prisoner. Details were very graphically given in *Life* magazine. And my mom, not having received a letter from her GI Joe in a very long time, thought he had fallen victim. Dad was a spotter; he went out ahead of the lines and called in the location of the Germans' heavily camouflaged big guns so that our planes and artillery could find and destroy them. He almost got taken out himself by the friendly fire of our own airmen a few times. After he returned home, he still had what today is known as PTSD. He broke into heavy sweats and woke up shaking at night. He lived in an apartment not far from LaGuardia airport in Queens, and planes coming in low over the apartment at late hours woke him from nightmares of being strafed. In my eyes, after he told this story to me in his later years, he was a hero.

By the time I came along, Mom and Dad had moved into an apartment in a part of Queens known as Sunnyside. I've always liked the songs "On the Sunny Side of the Street" and "Keep Your Sunny Side Up," and maybe that's why. Sunnyside is in western Queens, not far from the hospital on the opposite side of the East River where I was born. So although I'm a Manhattanite by birth, I crossed into one of New York's outer boroughs right away.

By the time I was four, we'd moved from Sunnyside. But my earliest recollections of life come from when we'd lived in another locale, a place farther east in Queens that my Uncle Edgar told me a joke about:

"What's the world's biggest plumbing problem? . . . Flushing New York!"

From the time I was four until just before my eighth birthday we lived in Flushing, home of baseball's Mets. My family and I—which during our four years in Flushing grew to include my brother, Gerry—lived a few miles from the site that later became Shea Stadium. I had a happy childhood there. I went to parochial school—St. Nicholas of Tolentine (not *the* St. Nicholas we all love so well, I later found out) for first and second grades. My cousins lived two blocks away. My Aunt Cat and Uncle Pat ran a candy store/luncheonette around the corner. I stopped by often. Cousin Denise would filch a few pieces of penny candy from behind the glass display case for me every so often. There was a German bar and beer garden next door to the candy store. The daughter of the family that owned it, Frieda Marie, became—as my mother would have me believe—my first girlfriend. I still have a picture around somewhere of Frieda Marie and me, at age five or so, skinny-dipping in a small inflatable backyard pool.

Other stores in that row around the corner included a butcher shop where I nearly always got a free slice of bologna when I went there with Mom, and a bakery where I nearly always got a free butter cookie. The butcher had a daughter . . . I wonder to this day if his bologna treats were bribes to try to lead me away from Frieda Marie and into the arms of *his* daughter.

Has this all gone to my head? Maybe.

In 1955, having scrimped and saved for enough years, my mom and dad decided to buy a house in the suburbs. We left Flushing and headed farther east on Long Island, about twenty miles from the city line. It was a tract house, one of about five hundred in the Cape Cod style. We put down roots there . . . in the town of Massapequa Park, named after the town of Massapequa just to its west—but so much more refined than Massapequa because it was an incorporated village. To prove my point: Massapequa was where those low-life Baldwin brothers, including Alec, their ringleader, grew up. But Alec went on to host *Saturday Night Live* many times. I didn't. Another town-name joke, commonly made in *both* Pequas: Mispronounce *Massapequa* and you get *Matzo-Pizza*. Many from both tribes known for those foods—matzo and pizza—were among my friends.

I went to public school in Massapequa from third through eighth grade. My brother, Gerry, went to parochial school, and suffered at the hands of the nuns. When my mom and dad told me they'd decided to send me to Catholic high school I quaked. My dad told me that I had been spoiled by my public school education and that he had strong morals because he'd attended a Catholic secondary school under the auspices of the Irish Christian Brothers, who didn't spare the garrison belt on seeming offenders. So in 1961, against my wishes, I began commuting back to Queens on school days via the Long Island Railroad, "The Route of the

Dashing Commuter," as the line's slogan went. I took the same trains as the suited captains of industry heading to the canyons of Wall Street. But I, age fourteen, traveled only as far as my school at Jamaica, Queens, a stop along the way.

I attended Archbishop Molloy High School in Jamaica, to be educated by the Marist Brothers. I lasted there a year and a half. Luckily, there was room back in the public schools of Massapequa for me to return there, and to bring my grades back up, among the likes of the Baldwins and their ilk.

After high school I moved to the ends of the earth. It was the farthest away from the New York City metro area I had ever lived, before moving to California. I spent four of the best years of my life at the State University of New York College at Geneseo, a truly idyllic outpost just west of New York's Finger Lakes. It was there that I met the love of my life, my now sainted Eleanor. We got into some innocent trouble every so often, staying out past dorm-curfew hours, going to keg parties, taking part in panty raids. We were the perfect match, both then and for forty-two years afterward. We were both born in New York City. Our pre-suburban early-childhood paths might have crossed, we later figured, at a pond in Jamaica Estates in Queens (Donald Trump's childhood neck of the woods), where our parents had taken us ice-skating. We had also been ships passing in the night many times, somewhere within the ten-mile span between our suburban hometowns, Massapequa Park and Huntington Station. But we didn't meet until we went to college in far-off Geneseo, three hundred and fifty miles away from our downstate suburban homes.

Eleanor and I had met several times during our first year at Geneseo, but didn't really hit it off until sophomore year. We became one of several campus couples who palled around in school and the valley during our years there. Western New York, especially around the Genesee Valley, is beautiful country . . . containing Letchworth Gorge, sometimes called the Grand Canyon of the East, and the town of Mt. Morris, birthplace of Francis Bellamy, author of the Pledge of Allegiance. Mt. Morris has more flags flying outside homes and more patriotic murals than anywhere else on earth, I believe.

When we and our coupled-up friends graduated, most of us wasted no time moving and marrying. Eleanor and I moved to Long Island. Our marriage had its ups and downs, but all in all it was the best we both could possibly have imagined at the *time* of our wedding—August 1969's Woodstock weekend. To the chagrin of my brother and Eleanor's sister the wedding was not held in Woodstock, but on Long Island. To this day neither of them has forgiven us.

I worked at MetLife, where I was called on for a bit of precision in reading and writing, one of several employees responsible for proofreading the new policy forms (those little booklets called life insurance policies by most people) prior to sending them to be published. Other companies manufacture widgets. My company manufactured words. I'm proud of the fact that in the late 1970s and early 1980s I took part in what was called the Plain English project, in which we were tasked with translating the policies' legalese into English that anyone with a tenth-grade education could read. My bosses didn't expect us to try very hard to make the wording in the policies completely grammatically correct. We who worked in Contract Bureau—who considered ourselves not very highly educated—were only expected to turn the policy clauses into words that the average Joe could understand.

I encountered the president of Met a few times and dined with our CEO once as well. I had a fairly good business relationship with the president's personal secretary. But unlike J. Pierpont Finch,

the lead character in my favorite musical and movie, *How to Succeed in Business without Really Trying*, I never made it to the boardroom, other than to deliver a few packets of paperwork—and unlike Bud Frump, the son of the World Wide Widgets Corporation President Biggley (of the same musical/movie), I wasn't fired either. I left MetLife on good terms after the Plain English project was completed, and much of Met's other work was outsourced during the 1980s.

In 1991 I began working for a government agency that shall remain unnamed. You, like nine out of ten folks, have doubtlessly waited in long lines at California's version of that agency. I moved up the ranks there to become a supervisor. For a time, I wanted to write a book about my years there and title it *Life in the Slow Line*. Eleanor even had written chapter headings for it, basing some of them on my moods when I got home each day. A good day was one in which as soon as I'd gotten home I'd pop open a brewski and sit at the piano and play Kenny Rogers' "The Gambler." A bad one was one in which I'd put on my boxing gloves and wail into an eighty-pound punching bag in the basement. The people I supervised at said agency were much more often the cause of that sparring than any of its customers. I put in twenty years there.

Other things happened in New York, some much sadder than Eleanor's and my younger siblings' having missed out on Woodstock. As a New Yorker, the events of September 11th, 2001, had a profound effect on me, although I didn't know anyone who died in the conflagration. I wasn't in the city that day, having left MetLife, which had offices in the World Trade Center, many years before. But I'd visited those offices several times, and I'd gone with family and friends to the observation deck on the one tower, and been to Windows on the World, the restaurant atop the other, a few times. My attachment to those buildings was very real, and I never could bring myself to visit the disaster site, other than driving by it once without stopping. I wanted to keep my good memories.

So now I'm up to the part of my story that's about my newfound home state and hometown. After a long illness, my missus passed away in 2011, and I went into a funk. I became a bit of a recluse. In 2013 I sold our home in the Long Island suburbs and downsized to a nearby apartment. Within a month after doing that, news arrived from my youngest son and his wife, who were living in the Golden State, that they were adopting a baby boy. Lo and behold. CJ, my first grandchild, was followed eight and a half months later by "Mr. Surprise," his brother TJ.

I left Long Island for good in November 2014, telling friends and family that I was seeking my fortune in the form of two gold nuggets in California. I got on a waiting list for a reasonably priced apartment down the street from my son's home in Alameda, then shopped in other towns in the East Bay for a place to wait until I got the call. I liked Martinez as my temporary hometown and lived there happily for a year and a half.

When I moved from Martinez to Alameda in June 2016, I decided to get more involved in life. I became active in the East Bay Regional Park District's volunteer docent program at the Crab Cove Visitors Center. I started coming to the current events class at Mastick whenever I could. Lately, I have been volunteering at Bingo at Mastick, and in February 2017 I decided to run for the volunteer job as recording secretary for the center's advisory board. I won the election, hands-down; I guess it helped being unopposed.

I'm very happy in Alameda. I bought a tricycle and try to get out and use it at least three times a week. Alameda has *got* to be the most bicycle-friendly town in California. You may see me around town on the trike. Give me plenty of room when you do! Sometimes I pedal like a house on fire when I'm in the street. When I'm on the paths in Crab Cove and Washington Park I take things slower. CJ and TJ are learning how to ride bikes now. They started last year with strider-bikes, bikes without pedals that are pushed along and stopped by foot power alone . . . like the Flintstones' car. In a sense, I bought the trike partly to be able to keep up with the little guys when they ride in Crab Cove or Washington Park.

Volunteering at Crab Cove is fun. More seniors should volunteer whenever they can. By splitting my volunteering between Crab Cove and Mastick, I serve both the newest generation and the folks of my own generation. It's interesting to watch the kids on school field trips to Crab Cove, and see their eyes light up when they catch on to something new about nature or their surroundings. I feel rewarded and blessed by seeing that. I feel rewarded and blessed by a lot of the folks at Mastick too. Nearly all of Mastick's members are pleasant and thoughtful, always willing to share a smile. I'm learning a lot from them about my new home too. I've always liked history, and this city has a lot that is interesting to me.

I like singing to my grandsons. Some of my favorites are Bing Crosby's "Swinging on a Star" and that classic children's song "On Top of Spaghetti." But my personal favorite is my new home state's official song, "I Love You California," especially this part:

It is here nature gives of her rarest.
It is Home Sweet Home to me,
And I know when I die I shall breathe my last sigh
For my sunny California.

Introduction

Harry Hopkins was concerned. As a top advisor to and speech-writer for FDR, he felt the media were doing a good job of reporting the impact of the Depression on the lives of ordinary people in urban areas. But how about citizens living in small towns and on farms in the wide countryside? He hired veteran AP reporter Lorena Hickok, age forty, and told her:

> Go talk with preachers and teachers, businessmen, workers, farmers. Go talk with the unemployed, those who are on relief and those who aren't. *And when you talk with them don't ever forget that by the grace of God you, I, any of our friends might be in their shoes* [emphasis added]. Tell me what you see and hear. All of it. Don't ever pull your punches. (David M. Kennedy, *Freedom from Fear: The American People in Depression and War, 1929–1945*)

Ms. Hickok took those instructions very seriously and provided some truly astonishing information. For example, she toured coal-mining towns in Appalachia and discovered that most children had never tasted dairy milk! It was likely her reporting, as communicated to the president by Hopkins, that prompted a widely quoted line in an FDR speech, lamenting that one-third of the nation was "ill-housed, ill-fed, ill-clothed."

Background

Agricultural prices dropped sharply during the post–World War I recession of 1920–21. The rest of the economy quickly recovered, but not farmers. Farm prices remained depressed throughout the ensuing decade, declining further during the steep descent into the Great Depression. Farmers allowed their crops to rot in the field because it did not pay to harvest them and transport them to market. The magnitude of market failure this represented was staggering: unharvested crops in the face of massive malnutrition and starvation.

John Oliver

My maternal grandfather, John Oliver, settled in the Ozark Mountains near the resort city of Eureka Springs, Arkansas, where he became prosperous. His base of operations was in a steep valley near a spring-fed stream. Ultimately, he acquired more than one thousand acres of dense forest, providing raw material for a lumber mill. His mill provided lumber for most of the early homes and a hotel in Eureka Springs. He also owned a brick kiln, and bricks from his kiln were used in the construction of the first building on the nearby campus of the University of Arkansas.

My grandfather outlived two wives, who gave him five sons and four daughters. Crystal, my mother, was his youngest child. He died in 1931. His property was divided among his offspring. Mother was awarded two hundred and forty acres of forest, rocks, and poisonous snakes on a gentle slope of Swain Mountain. A wagon trail provided access from a nearby road leading to Eureka Springs.

The John and Crystal Guinn Family

My dad, John, was semiliterate. He completed eighth grade, but he could barely read and write. However, he was good with arithmetic; he could do basic calculations accurately in his head. He also applied the Pythagorean theorem in carpentry work. He called it the 6-8-10 rule.

Mother dropped out of high school in her junior year to take care of her ailing mother.

My parents were living on a rented farm in central Oklahoma when my brother and I were born, Dwight in April 1925, and me in late November 1928. Sometime after my grandfather's death, after auctioning off most of our household possessions, farm equipment, and livestock (one of the smartest things my parents did was to slaughter one or two of their cows and can the beef), my dad loaded our remaining possessions into a covered wagon and traveled more than two hundred miles to Eureka Springs. He sought temporary shelter with Crystal's sister and her husband, who had a secure job as a rural mail carrier. Dad left the wagon and horses there, and returned to fetch his family.

In late fall or early winter we were living in an old rented house on a country road. Heat came from a potbellied woodstove. One cold night the roof caught fire. Somehow neighbors converged, formed a bucket brigade from the well pump to the burning roof, and extinguished the fire. Of course we now had a leaky roof!

When weather permitted, my dad traveled to the inherited property to clear land and start constructing shelter. He completed a chicken house by late spring. We moved some bedding and a woodstove into that and lived there while he felled cedar trees, had the logs milled, and constructed a four-room house. There wasn't time to allow the lumber to season properly, so the siding shrank and left large cracks. We covered them with slats.

Some eight-foot two-by-fours left from construction were stacked neatly in a side yard. One day some neighboring cousins were visiting, and we were having great fun running and jumping over the lumber. I tripped on a stub and fell face-first, hitting the bridge of my nose on a corner of a two-by-four. An artery was severed and blood gushed out. Fortunately, Dad had delayed leaving to work in the fields. He held me in one arm, grabbed the lower half of my nose, forced it upward, and maintained strong pressure for several minutes. Meanwhile, Mother prepared some cloth strips (no tape available). These were used to construct a Rube Goldberg–type bandage to maintain the pressure. Of course, I had to breathe through my mouth. The results of their efforts were amazing: My nose is almost perfectly straight, with a very faint scar. Dad saved my life, and I am forever grateful.

Next Dad set about clearing the land for crops. Logs had to be dragged off and stumps removed. Removing stumps is incredibly difficult. We now had just one horse, a large black gelding named Prince. Using plow, axe, pick, and shovel, dirt was removed around the stump and surface roots cut. Then it gets to be very difficult because the stump must be separated from the taproot. This was done by hooking the nose of a plow under the stump and urging Prince to use all the strength at his command. Meanwhile, Dad had to use all of his own strength to bear down on the plow handles to prevent the plow from flipping forward. It would be difficult to imagine a more difficult task, and it had to be repeated several times.

The first crop he planted on this virgin soil was strawberries. Picking the ripe berries in the spring involved all family members, plus a female neighbor from a nearby farm. Dad hired a truck and driver to transport the harvest to a regional market in a nearby city. I doubt that the revenue was sufficient to cover the cost, because the next year we tried a different crop, tomatoes.

As the crop ripened, we picked, crated, and loaded it onto a one-horse wagon equipped with rubber-tired wheels, but no brakes. We took it to a canning factory in the nearby village of Clifty, with Dwight and me along for the ride. An accident happened on one trip. We were traveling along a moderately steep downslope when the harness strap around Prince's hip broke. Prince had to move much faster to avoid being run over. Dad skillfully guided him into the bar ditch so the wheels would grind against the side of the ditch and bring the wagon to a halt. Dad poached some wire from a nearby fence and repaired the damaged harness well enough to proceed.

When we delivered the last load of the harvest to the factory, we experienced dramatic evidence of the conditions described in the "Background" section above: Dad went to the factory office to collect payment for multiple deliveries and found a notice on the door that the company had declared bankruptcy. Our income for that year was zero!

How did we make it through the winter? Cedar posts could be sold for five cents each. Dad had a crosscut saw designed for one person but with a detachable handle on the narrow end for use by a second person. He would work all day felling trees and cutting trunks into post lengths. Large trunks could be split into more than one post. Dwight and I would join him after school. Fortunately, Dwight was right-handed and I was left-handed, so it worked well to have us positioned on opposite sides of the saw handle.

The church we attended when possible used a one-room school building in Clifty for Sunday worship services. Church leaders decided they had cash reserves sufficient to construct a separate building. Dad had acquired carpentry skills in his youth, so he was hired to help with construction. This would help bail us out from the two fruitless years of farming. We did not own a car, so he walked about five miles each way daily. The job lasted two or three months.

Shortly afterward, our Oklahoma relatives notified us of a large-road construction project in the western part of the state. It was likely financed by one of FDR's New Deal programs. The job required the use of dump trucks to haul gravel. Dad used the bank credit he had established in the village of Meeker to purchase a truck and equip it with a dump bed. We moved to Weatherford, near the project, and took up residence in a rented furnished house. It was summer when we arrived and the project extended into the fall. Dwight and I enrolled in the local schools. When the project was completed, we moved back to Swain Mountain, with the family finances much improved.

Dad then equipped the truck with a flat bed and started soliciting hauling jobs. He soon became quite busy. Frequently the jobs were long distance, requiring long work hours. After a few months, even as a child, I noticed that Dad had become more slender.

After one or two years we moved to a farmhouse on a country road not far away from Swain Mountain. It included a chicken house that we used and a barn that we did not. We had a black tomcat named Midnight. He would go hunting in the woods behind the barn each morning and return in the evening. One evening I spied him in the distance, and he was dragging something. He would pull it a few feet, then stop and rest. He finally arrived, proudly displayed a huge rattlesnake, and walked away. He obviously wanted his family to see what he had accomplished.

We made the fabled Depression-era California trip in 1941. Our destination was Redding, where Mother's sister and brother lived. Shasta Dam was under construction, providing work for many carpenters. Dad worked there, but just for a short time. The work was extraordinarily dangerous. I remember watching from below, and the workmen were so high up they looked like midgets scrambling along suspended scaffolds.

My parents searched the want ads and saw an opportunity to manage a dairy herd a short distance east of Yreka. A small bungalow was provided. Dad's first love was farming, especially working with animals. So we moved again in the early summer of that year.

The herd was fairly large, so vacuum milking machines were used. Teats still had to be "stripped" by hand to finish the job. Dwight and I helped with that. I must mention another animal experience. We had a dog that made the mistake of attacking a porcupine. He acquired a nose full of needles that Dad had to remove with pliers.

Mother became quite lonely because there were no close neighbors and no church denomination that had earned my parents' loyalty. Dwight was even more dissatisfied because he had become close friends with a high school classmate in Huntsville, Arkansas. So we first moved back to Redding, thinking Dwight might link up with a friend there. Nope. He was still unhappy, and Dad was constantly afraid he might run away. We then moved back to Arkansas, this time to Huntsville, where the high school was. Soon thereafter, war mobilization, following the bombing of Pearl Harbor, marked the end of the Great Depression. We had survived . . . much better than millions of other rural residents. There were times when we had a steady diet of beans and potatoes for lunch and dinner, but Dwight and I never went to bed hungry.

Mabel and Willard

This middle-aged couple lived in a cottage a bit farther up on Swain Mountain. Willard had been managing the only hotel in Shawnee, Oklahoma, a short distance from our farm, when the Great Depression struck. The hotel went bankrupt and Willard lost his job. The couple also likely lost money in the financial market crash of 1929. The cottage they had been using as a vacation hideaway now became their permanent residence. We learned from Mabel, a frequent visitor, that Willard was so depressed he would not eat. He finally stopped short of starving to death.

Mabel had been a garden club–attending, chain-smoking socialite in Shawnee. But she adapted to the extreme change of fortune much better than Willard. She was resilient. They continued to receive a small amount of investment income monthly. She hired someone to build a chicken house and pigpen, and housed the acquired creatures accordingly. She planted a garden. She had a great sense of humor and was a great conversationalist, notwithstanding her chain-smoking habit.

Mabel was childless, so she took an interest in Dwight and me. She wanted us to have some non-rural experiences. Had we ever heard of ice cream sundaes? No. So she managed to hitch a ride for us to nearby Springdale, take us to a drugstore, and give us a treat. I chose chocolate. When *Snow White and the Seven Dwarfs* came to a theater in Eureka Springs, she made sure we saw it. My parents had no way of knowing about such luxurious things.

Mabel and Willard ultimately purchased our land, on contract, for eight hundred dollars. The US Forestry Service built a fire lookout tower on their property, and Willard was hired as a lookout. He would climb to the top a few times each day and scan the area for signs of a fire—an interesting change from managing a hotel! Economic conditions have consequences.

Hershel and Family

These folks were squatters. They lived in a one-room unpainted shack on the adjacent property roughly one and a half miles from our house. Hershel was illiterate. His wife, whose name I don't recall, had completed fifth grade. They had a girl about my age and a younger boy. Hershel tried to make a living by making and selling railroad ties. He had a one-person crosscut saw to fell oak trees and a broad axe to shape them into ties. He had no way to deliver them, so he probably had to sell them at a considerable discount to a trucker.

One spring we were hit with a prolonged, massive rainstorm. After several days Hershel and family appeared at our door and requested shelter. It was early in the morning, so Mom prepared breakfast, featuring fried eggs. The children had never tasted eggs in any form. The boy, about age six, kept requesting more. He consumed a total of nine eggs! Millions of children, especially in rural areas, suffered malnutrition, or worse, during the Depression. This case was painfully close by.

Uncle Fred Oliver

Uncle Fred's life offers a different slant on the Great Depression. He was a farmer and trader who had a college degree and knew how to take advantage of the economic circumstances. He lived in a comfortable house located on a flat pasture about two miles from our Swain Mountain residence.

There were numerous auctions among financially distressed farmers. Frequently farm animals that had not been properly fed were sold. Fred would bid on these, but he knew when to stop. He would acquire such animals at a low price, feed them well, then sell them for a much higher price, not by auction but by advertising. He spent considerable time mingling with area farmers in downtown Eureka Springs every Saturday. There he could advertise his live-stock by word of mouth and acquire intelligence about upcoming auctions or other buying opportunities. I do not think Fred took advantage of anyone. All transactions in which he was involved were mutually advantageous to both buyer and seller. He did not take advantage of individuals; he took advantage of the circumstances.

Fred and his wife had a teenage daughter. He, like Mabel, also took an interest in Dwight and me. He occasionally took us with him on his Saturday trips to Eureka Springs. I was especially fascinated by visiting the Basin Street (resort) Hotel, which had a fast-flowing stream that passed through the lobby. It was fun to watch the fish swim by.

Final Comments

This country came perilously close to repeating the Great Depression experience in 2008. What saved us from that fate were the decisive and skillful actions that Federal Reserve Chairman Ben Bernanke implemented. He would have been more successful had it not been for what he called "headwinds" caused by a clue-less Congress. Dr. Bernanke should be awarded a medal.

On a personal note, I experienced the Great Depression during my formative years and it profoundly impacted me and defines who I am.

Who's an Alamedan and Other True Crime Stories

Stanley Hallmark

Who's an Alamedan is a matter of perspective. Those born here deny the status to everyone else. I have a lower standard: If you have been here for more than thirty years, you may call yourself an Alamedan. For me that thirty-year cutoff point means you remember the Naval Air Station, raised kids, fought with the school district, and heard Buena Vista called *Bona Vista* and Versailles called *Versallyese*, both recognized as acceptable. Also, you have been here long enough to absorb some of the history of the town. When you first got here, for example, you probably wondered why some streets were one hundred and sixty feet wide, and then you learned that streetcars and railroad trains once ran down the middle of them.

I have run into millennials I will grant Alamedan status because they are romantically in love with our old Victorians and with the old newsstand on Park and Santa Clara. They think we are quaint and special. Yes we are quaint but also cosmopolitan, and we have old people and families with little children, little towheads and little ones with dreadlocks and headscarves, all of them lovely children—I know this because I occupy that newsstand at Park and Santa Clara four hours a day and see a cross section of Alameda walk by. I mention the children because they always see me and the parents don't. These young families are on their way to becoming Alamedans.

When my wife died in 2013, I kind of had to reinvent myself. After thirty-five years of marriage, I was pretty lost. I was used to making decisions for two and it now it had become one. My first reaction was to bury myself in my love of science and math. I became a hermit. I was not a hermit at heart though. I found a social outlet at bars, among artists and engineers, accountants and graphic designers. I learned that if you talk to strangers they talk back, and what they say expands your world.

I realize in retrospect that I have intertwined my life with observations of Alameda because I rarely leave the city limits. This would suggest I have everything I need here, but I smoke a pipe and would like a good pipe shop. I guess I've had enough travel. In my lifetime, I've toured the US and visited several European countries, plus an all-expenses-paid trip to Vietnam, courtesy of Uncle Sam. In a later occupation I was a private investigator, and there were days when I drove up and down the interstate, logging two hundred miles a day on the job. So I guess I really have had it with travel.

Another interest of mine now is my granddaughter, whom I raised from age five to age eleven and taught to defend herself verbally. She has turned into a champion lawyer, to her mother's great dismay—the simplest request like "clean your room" results in a one-hour negotiation about what constitutes cleaning your room; what are the time limits for this job; can some of the task be done tomorrow; and, finally, what criteria are going to be used to judge whether the room is clean or not.

Another aspect of my aging life is being attacked by people who want to come to my aid when I don't need it. If I stop on the street and bend forward to light my pipe, three people see an old man who is having a heart attack. I have to reassure them that I am in good health—not my exact words, to be honest.

I am very attached to my community. They are a gutsy bunch that have moved beyond bake sales and real estate agents. They have voted to make Alameda a sanctuary city, and called for an impeachment investigation of Donald Trump regarding potential conflicts of interest. I now realize that as I move closer to community so has the country: people are realizing that the power and strength of this country resides in the people, not in senators or presidents.

The issue of citizenship became a topic in my second career (between the military and being a private investigator), in corrections. I was first a prison guard and later a probation officer. People convicted of felonies are denied the right to vote, but most of the guys who were convicted didn't think that was important. So I began to explain to them the extent of that loss. The unintended consequence of my actions was to create awareness of local empowerment and how to engage it. I was suddenly holding civics classes as a probation officer, and it seemed to be called for. In the case of those men, bringing them closer to an awareness of community was what they needed. If you see a community as your friends, you don't steal from them or hurt them.

I quickly learned that unemployment was a big factor in the lives of many convicted criminals. At first I simply sympathized, and then I decided I might be able to do something about it. My first effort came about when I learned that the heavy equipment operators' union was under attack for not hiring minorities. I called the union and said hey, I've got some people who are minorities and are good prospects. I went through my directory and found some who had truck-driving experience, gave them my business card, and sent them over there. Some were taken into the apprentice program. What pleased me most was that one of the guys accepted was an Eskimo. He and his family had been moved, by the Bureau of Indian Affairs at the government's request, from their land on St. Lawrence Island, in the Bering Strait, and relocated to Richmond, California, because it had a whaling station, which, it was hoped, would suffice for the family's needs. No one bothered to check out that the little Richmond station cut up only one whale every six months, and no whaling ships operated on San Francisco Bay. So an Eskimo family was shipped five thousand miles and twenty-one centuries in time, to no advantage. I was overwhelmed with joy when the union took this kid because I had no idea what to do with him otherwise.

My third occupation, being a private investigator, shortened my life, aging me twice as fast as I should have. The case that affected me the most was one in which I worked for an attorney who was being plagued by a Devil, or I should say a be-Deviler, someone who secretly acts maliciously toward you. At that time, many private investigators got cases like this. Most were easy to solve because they followed a pattern: The "Devil" was usually someone from the person's past who began showing up around the person surreptitiously. He might begin by pretending to bump into the person at a supermarket or a coffee shop the person frequented. Then things escalated; for example, he might put sugar in the gas tank of the victim's car. In this case, the Devil found an open window at the victim's home, put a garden hose through it, and turned on the water, flooding the living room.

I was first contacted about this case at the point at which the Devil had spread some slanderous, salacious material about the attorney. The material in evidence included a photo of the attorney's three-year-old daughter without clothes, taken by a family member in the backyard on a summer day. Accompanying the photo was a typewritten message claiming that the attorney was a child pornographer. Envelopes containing copies of the photo and message had been delivered to all of the attorneys in the immediate neighborhood and, the following day, to all the judges in the superior court. The most troubling aspect of this evidence was that the photo of the child had been stolen from the attorney's house, which meant the Devil had entered the house and no one had known it. The fear this realization generated was massive.

One night the Devil was seen near the house and he ran away, and a pair of eyeglasses was found and presumed to be his. These glasses and the envelopes and photocopies of the photo and note were the only physical evidence we had.

I set to work on the glasses. They had prescription lenses, and the prescription was common to middle-age men forty and over. It was a sort of fingerprint, narrowing the group of potential suspects somewhat. My client, the attorney, who I'd allowed to have a little too much involvement in the investigation, had already spoken to the optical society and gotten cooperation for a search of local opticians' files. The attorney sent us some office assistants to help search the records. One of them acted like he did a records search every day before breakfast, and he was a speed demon; he began eliminating prescriptions faster than the reflexes on a squirrel. I suggested that everybody slow down, but he insisted he could read fifty prescriptions in the blink of an eye. The search of these records went on for three days. We then began searching small optometry offices.

Simultaneously, we began to get an artist's sketch of what the Devil looked like. In the course of initial interviews with possible witnesses, we realized that the Devil must have been posing as a mailman. It was clear that the envelopes in which the photos and notes were delivered had been previously used, and that the envelopes had been delivered by hand. I believe we had only two good witnesses to the phony mailman, who came back to the house and was also seen by the attorney. But none of the artist's sketches looked like anyone the attorney knew.

I continued to work on the glasses. I got a crash course in eyeglass construction. I bought the five most commonly used blank lenses and started making phone calls to the companies that made them. Three were eliminated because the companies also sold lenses to people who made microscopes; the blanks were too expensive to be used in a cheap pair of glasses like the ones the Devil had left behind. That left me with two companies, and I began conversations with them, asking how I could tell which blank was used on this pair. Both companies told me that the lenses would be too small to tell anything from. A few days later I got a call from an engineer at one of the companies. He told me that the lenses his company made had a different inner arc from the one the other company made—on the lenses he made it was twenty degrees and on his competitor's it was twenty-five degrees. Further, the arc would remain no matter how much the lens was cut down. I took the Devil's glasses to an optician, who determined that the arc was twenty-five degrees. I had the company that made the lenses.

Next I contacted the company's sales staff. The company was nationwide, but fortunately only sold to one place in Northern California. I agreed to write a letter outlining my request and the reasons for it, and to include a hold-harmless declaration to clear the company of any liability in the case. The company then verified my credentials. Finally, they told me what I wanted to know: they had only one retail outlet in my area. That retailer then gave the authorization to inspect its records.

Meanwhile, the attorney wanted to find this Devil so quickly he urged me to follow up every lead immediately. This wasn't the way

I would run an investigation, but as I mentioned earlier I'd let the attorney to become a little too involved, and now I was paying the price. So while I allowed myself to be diverted to other leads, the speed-demon assistant searching the records missed the Devil's prescription.

Speculation at the time was leaning toward the idea that the Devil was someone connected to the attorney's wife, who was a therapist. A handful of her ex-patients were tracked down. An adult bookstore claimed that a pretend mailman was a regular customer, so stakeout was put on that lead. There were leads that a weird guy who was a regular user of the library reading room looked like our composite sketch, so the library was also watched. A time-lapse camera was put in the attorney's office and processed daily. In the middle of all of this, I was requested to present the case to amateur sleuths who were friends of the family.

I had contacted the postal inspectors because our suspect could have been a real mailman, but no one in our area was on their radar. I had the envelopes our Devil had recycled for use, all stamped with postage-metering machines. Almost the only source of such envelopes was one company, and after hours of begging them to give me the manufacturer's address they did. Tracking down the original recipients of these envelopes disclosed that they all had post office boxes at a small local-annex post office. The postal inspectors allowed me to copy the names of the seventy-two box holders, but none of them were familiar to the attorney.

Welcome to the world of the private investigator.

Then things nearly turned deadly. The attorney was now as obsessed with the Devil as the Devil was with him. One night the obsessions collided: The Devil was prowling around the house and tripped an alarm. The attorney slipped out of the house with a gun. Not having the heart to be a killer, he jumped the Devil, who also had a gun and managed to shoot the attorney and escape. Again, the attorney didn't recognize him.

All leads went dead. In desperation we made a flyer, which resulted in a woman calling and identifying the Devil, and the police moved in and arrested him. Tragically, this guy had been identified five days into the investigation, but the evidence had been ignored. At that time, after collecting all the physical evidence, we had decided to hold a confessional meeting between the attorney and me—a confessional meeting means having a fuller conversation along the lines of answering the question, "Who would do this to you?" It's not an easy thing to do. The attorney had to review every one of his actions and consider whom he could have possibly wronged or who might think he had, so that that person had become his enemy.

After three hours of talking through several social situations, I pointed out again, for the fourth time, that the slander was aimed at him not personally, but as an attorney. I finally said, "Don't you have some attorney who hates you from the courtroom?" He said, "No!" Then he said, "Well, there was one guy, who defended himself in a suit claiming that his dogs constituted a nuisance." The attorney had represented the plaintiff in the case. I said this could be our guy. My client said no, that man was short and very fat and looked nothing like the artist's sketches of our fake mailman.

It turned out that the guy who was the Devil had lost something like a hundred and fifty pounds since the dog-nuisance trial, something that rarely happens and that also dramatically changes one's appearance. The woman who had responded to the flyer we'd put out had said the magic words: that the man she thought it was had these annoying dogs.

That turned out to be the end of a very long, chaotic trail. The case lasted almost a year. And it did me in for a while.

What I have learned from both books and people are two things: First: Everything is in motion, from the atoms in a table to the planets and the sun racing through the galaxy—social events and people change, and nothing waits for you. Second, and this comes mostly from listening to folks who talk to me at the newsstand: Don't be so damn certain of your position, or of whatever perspective you have, that it might close your mind and prevent you from talking to others. Talk to people who disagree with you. You might learn something.

The Tropical Rain Forest

Paul Hauser

In 1968 I went to work as a cartographer for the Inter American Geodetic Survey based out of the Panama Canal Zone. I took the job feeling like a pioneer working on the frontier of the unknown world. In the age of airplanes and space travel, the impenetrable jungles/tropical rain forests of Central and South America were still blank spaces on the world map. It was largely undeveloped land, including vast tracks of, arguably, some of the most inhospitable terrain on earth. My first mapping party assignment was to explore and identify all known features on the Platano River in Honduras, starting on the Caribbean Sea and ending a hundred miles into the unmapped tropical rain forest. On July 30, 1502 Christopher Columbus first saw this river and went on to claim all of the territory, now known as Honduras, in the name of his sovereigns, Ferdinand II of Aragon and Isabella I of Castile. The area was designated in 1982 as a United Nations World Heritage Site and named the Rio Platano Biosphere Reserve.

The most striking thing about working in that tropical rain forest—the thing that shocked me—was the color. There was none of the modulation, the melting of one shade into another. So slight were the differences in values of the various greens that it was almost impossible for me to get a photograph of the tropical foliage. The ever-present background was an almost undifferentiated green. And splatted all over it, like a postimpressionist painting, were masses of color in the most vivid contrasts: yellow, crimson, green, and dazzling white. And this was one of the things that surprised me about that tropical rain forest—it was immensely beautiful. Somehow the filtered light reduced what might have been unspeakable gaudiness to a rich, real harmony.

Traveling inland we frequently encountered a dizzying variety of vines. Some killed the host tree they grew upon not by strangulation, but by smothering. Their leaves grew with a precision that seemed intelligent: the leaves lay flat on the bark of the tree, overlapping each other about a quarter of an inch, until they encircled the doomed trunk in an airtight sheath.

Lush was not a strong enough word to describe what we saw and yet I could not think of another word to describe the vegetation. It certainly was prolific.

Over a period of time I came to understand that death came to all things in the tropical rain forest, not so much from an extraneous accident as from the sheer pressure of birth and growth. The new was pushing into life with such haste, such insistence, that nothing had a chance to reach a ripe maturity.

Occasionally we came upon a stream curving its way through the thick vegetation. Since the rivers and streams drained the tropical rain forests, they became the lifelines for the indigenous people living along its banks. There was very little circulation of commodities beyond those navigable waters. They were the quickest means of transportation into and out of the tropical rain forest.

So intense was the vegetable life of the tropical rain forest that most large animals were crowded out. Yet the tropical rain forest was home to many endangered species. Monkeys and birds of every description inhabited the overhead areas. You might walk a day or two without seeing any and then be overwhelmed with the variety of creatures above you. Walking along a trail one day I encountered a three-foot-long white nosed coati. It seemed as surprised as I was for the encounter. A glimpse of the Scarlet Macaws overhead or the Blue Morpho Butterfly gliding through the air was breath taking. One night while in a small clearing we listened to Jaguars making a repetitive coughing sound, followed by an occasional vocalized mew and grunt. Then there were the snakes, poisonous and non-poisonous, slithering on the floor of the tropical rain forest or hanging on branches. Crocodiles hid in the dark waters. They all blended so well with the vegetation and terrain that they were nearly invisible. More than once I nearly stepped on a fer-de-lance snake, and I almost walked into a pea-green pit viper wrapped around an eye-level tree branch. Both of those snakes could kill a human quickly.

But if the plants had preempted the ground space to the exclusion of larger animal forms, the air was free for abundant insect life. You could not walk fifteen minutes without crossing the trail—a well-beaten path—of some variety of ant or bug. Moths, beetles, bugs of every kind and description abounded in the rain forest. Mosquitoes transmitted a variety of diseases, including yellow fever, dengue, encephalitis, elephantiasis, and most famously malaria. The torment and menace of bats, snakes, mosquitoes, intolerable tiny gnats, and stinging ants with all their accompanying diseases and fevers caused us at times to be miserable. That said, of all the ways a man could die in this tropical rain forest, what we feared most was being disoriented and lost.

I remember so vividly my days of mapping in those densely overgrown areas with their overhead canopies formed by tall trees that prevented most of the sunlight from entering. I think everyone who has ever entered a tropical rain forest has felt its personality. No one can escape the spell of its beauty, a beauty rich and luxuriant and threatening, a beauty supported by dread. Hardly loveable, but infinitely fascinating.

Excerpts from this story were taken from the author's 2016 Amazon.com book entitled, I'm Always Going Somewhere: Mapping in Latin America for the Inter American Geodetic Survey.

SAVED BY GRACE

Usha Muliyil Helm

I was nine when a young woman came to the gate. She was so poor her rags barely covered her pregnant belly and her legs. She held a baby in her arms, which she offered to me. It was my very first decision. I had lost a baby brother from nephritis, my mother's doing, and my mother had another baby, my little sister. She was a mother whom I still have trouble thinking of as Mother. I was her first-born, and my uncle, who was unmarried at the time, loved me and saved me. This is why I am alive, alone in a foreign land.

That young woman was beautiful and about to die with both her babes. I knew my mother would hex that infant the way she had my baby brother, so I turned my head away, praying someone else would take her baby.

Mother love is like God's love. Some people have it from their mothers. Others, like the Lord Jesus and Buddha, seek it from God. Father Damien gave love to the lepers in Molokai and Kalawao, in Hawaii. He became one of them and died of the most virulent form of the disease. Mother Marianne worked almost twice as long in Molokai with her nuns. She was a great woman.

I started dreaming of mother love when I lost that baby that had been offered to me, so soon after losing my brother. When I was ten I had to take care of two babies. It was wartime, and men and money were being sent to the war zone.

I had two babies instead of dolls to play with, but my mother took them away from me. She told them I was not a good person, and she treated me as a scapegoat for her own wrongdoing.

Satan is at work when people go to war, although they do not talk of that evil spirit. I do not like armies and navies and bomber planes. I saw that starving young mother. I was starved by my mother for fully ten years of my life, and I used to climb a tree and talk to Jesus, and ask Him to help me.

The Lord saved me. This past year has been a period of grace because I follow the Gospel, and Vedanta, as taught to me by one of the best teachers in the Bay Area, and the *I Ching*, the Chinese *Book of Changes*, blessed by Confucius and Carl Jung. I follow these to understand what God wants me to do.

My Early Childhood in the "Big" House

Virginia Leung Jang

"**B**aba, what are these? Do we have to cook them?" Flora looked puzzled at those strange-looking red balls, called *ping guor,* in Father's hand.

Father had just returned from his business trip to Hong Kong, our hometown, in the fall of 1945, after the end of the Second World War, and he had brought back some Red Delicious apples imported from America. Flora, my four-year-old younger sister, had never seen any apples in her entire life. But how could she? She was born just before the war, when Japan took over Hong Kong from the British in 1941. I was about two then. During those dark days we had been deprived of all luxuries and imported goods.

As the war went on, commerce and transportation between Hong Kong, China, and the rest of the world were disrupted. My father was forced to close his businesses. How he was going to support a large young family remained a big question. Then food supplies became scarce and the prices escalated. In 1942, with his family facing starvation, my father decided to move us to Guangzhou (Canton), China, where he had found a place to live and some business connections. We took a long boat ride, about eighty miles, north from the mouth of Pearl River to Guangzhou, the largest city in Southern China. At least in Guangzhou there were farming villages close by and food supplies were more stable. Guangzhou had been lost to Japan years earlier, and since then had been under a puppet Chinese provisional government established by the Japanese invaders.

We moved to a "big" Chinese-style, two-story house on *Yil Wah Dai Guy* (Yil Wah Big Street), and became housesitters for the next three and a half years while the wealthy owners were away in Malaysia. What a treat, free rent! And what a change from living in the crowded flat in Hong Kong. The house seemed to have all sorts of space and different rooms for us to run around in. There was a little courtyard in the middle of the house, and in the back was a staircase leading to the second floor where the bedrooms were. In the front of the house there was another staircase, leading to a study and a rooftop patio. My older brother, Fila, age five then, was just thrilled to death. He could run up and down the stairs. He found the perfect escape route to use when he got into trouble with our parents. "Come and catch me. I can run faster than you. Ha, ha, ha, you'll never find me. You won't know where I'll be hiding!" he'd say, laughing.

Although we had electricity in most of the house, the power supply was intermittent at best. We used kerosene lanterns or oil lamps at night, and I remember those oil lamps well. They looked like tall green pottery candlesticks with a little dish on the top for oil and a wick. I was fascinated by the *dung sum,* the wick; it wasn't like anything I had seen before. I only know that it was made of some kind of plant material that is used in Chinese herbal medicine. The *dung sum* looks like a short, thick, white string, light as a feather and spongy, and it soaks up oil like cotton wool.

We didn't like the oil lamps. The flickering gave us an eerie feeling, and we were afraid of ghosts. At night, Flora and I would follow Ah Samm, our long-time helper and nanny, around in the big dark house. We slept with her for a while. Sometimes, when we were mischievous, she would say to us, "You better be good; otherwise the *au woo ma* will come and get you." We didn't know exactly what she meant by that. We presumed that the *au woo ma* must be an ugly, mean, old woman, like the big bad wolf, who would come after naughty little children. After the warning, we would calm down, but that made us even more afraid to go out and about in the dark.

Shortly after we moved into the house, we were startled by the drumming noises, *dog, dog, dog,* out in the street in the middle of the night. I jumped up, "What is that noise, Ah Samm?"

"Oh, it is only the *da gown lo.* Never mind, go back to sleep."

Next morning, mother told us what the *da gown lo* was—the night watchman, like the town crier. She explained to us that before the clock became a regular household timepiece, it was tradition to signal the time at night. The watchman would go on his beat and sound his drum every few hours. He also watched out for fires and thieves, and he would beat the drum when needed. When he signaled the "fifth round," it would be time to get up.

Next to our house was the Number 27 Primary School, where my two older sisters, Julie and Selena, went. But poor Lora, my second-eldest teenage sister, had to walk a long way to go to the junior high school. There were no buses around. There was also no kindergarten or nursery school, so Fila, Flora, and I were stuck in the house all the time. We were just preschoolers. We had no toys or dolls either, and we had to learn to entertain ourselves. Sometimes, my older sisters would teach us to play Chinese Jacks with little stones we found in the street. And I would practice playing with the stones all day long.

Fila was lucky. He had a bag of marbles to keep him busy. He drew some circles in the courtyard, and he shot the marbles into the circles like shooting pool. When he got tired of playing by himself he would say to me, "Come, I will let you play with my marbles. You play in that corner."

"No, I don't want to play."

"But I want you to play with me."

"O-kay." I yielded to his demand. Although I wanted to touch those precious marbles of his, the scars on my head reminded me what happened when I played with him last. It was damned if I do and damned if I don't. What was the point of playing with him? I was doomed to lose; he was a sharpshooter. And if I ever won, would he be willing to part with his marbles?

In the front entrance of our house was a black sliding wooden gate with horizontal bars from top to bottom. During the summer days, my mother would shut the gate and leave the door open to let the breeze in. I found my monkey bar! I could do big-sister duty and keep Flora busy while all other girls were in school. Flora and I would climb up and down the bars as if they were branches on a tall oak tree. We sat on the bar and dangled our legs, and we sang and giggled like we were on a swing. I felt I had wings flying up in the air. We were up there in our own space and nobody could get us! Sometimes, when nobody was watching, I would hang myself upside down like a bat with my legs gripping onto the bar! Flora couldn't do that; she was just a little girl. "Let's see who can climb faster," I said to Flora.

"Okay. I can climb fast too."

We raced, climbing up and down the bars. But Flora had to climb the bars slowly, moving her right foot first onto the next bar and then her left foot. I just jumped right up the ladder and slid back down, and of course it wasn't like playing with Fila—now I won for a change.

During the days in Guangzhou I spent the most time with my father, who was about forty then. He was a businessman, but commerce was not very active. He didn't have regular work and hardly had any business entertainment. But father was always an outgoing, gregarious, and resourceful man. It was his courage and business savvy that led us through this dark period. He made money by trading goods and brokering services to put food on the table. When times were bad, my mother told me years later, he had to trade in her dowry and jewelry so we wouldn't go hungry. And we never did.

My Father's favorite hobby was eating and trying out different foods; it was evident by his weight. He was of medium height but was a heavy man by Chinese standards. One day, he brought a large old-fashioned coffee grinder and some wheat home. He told Flora and me, "I am going to make *mein* (noodles)."

"*Ho yair, ho yair.* Oh, goody, goody." We were happy to find something new for entertainment. He fastened the coffee grinder onto a bed board and placed the board on the large ping-pong table in the living room. "Ah, I want you two to sit on the other end and don't jump. I need you to hold the board down. And keep your hands off the side of the board."

"Okay." We climbed onto the table and sat on the board with our legs crossed. I sat in the back with my arms around Flora to make sure she wouldn't touch the board. The board bounced up and down as father ground the wheat into coarse brown flour. We thought that bumpy ride was fun since it was our first seesaw experience. Father then sifted the flour and turned it into homemade noodles. I still don't know how he managed to do that, but they were delicious. On another occasion, we followed him around while he made soap from lard and some caustic solution. There were other experiments I learned from him that I would not have been exposed to if I had been in school.

In our kitchen we had a perfect, fuel-efficient, brass portable stove and water boiler, all in one, called *won sui lo*. This was like a family treasure. On one side it had a burner for the rice cooker, and one for the *wok* on the opposite side. The burners were connected with a tube to the water boiler in the middle. When we cooked, the heat from the two burners would spread through the tube to the center to boil water for drinking or bathing.

During those days, we had to use firewood for fuel and straw for kindling. They put out a lot of soot and smoke that blackened the kitchen walls and ceiling. When spring came the days were miserably warm and humid, and even the walls and the ceiling would sweat. Then the moisture mixed with the soot on the kitchen ceiling, and pretty soon there would be a collection of black droplets, like soy sauce, hanging on the ceiling ready to drop. I was afraid to go into the kitchen then. I didn't want to have soy sauce rain on my head!

In late spring 1945, the Allied Forces began fighting with the Japanese in Southern China. American army planes started bombing the Japanese military facilities and transportation routes around Guangzhou. The bombers came at all times, night and day, and the siren went on constantly. Whenever it rang, my parents would warn us, "Turn off all the lights; go downstairs and stay under the ping-pong table. Hurry!"

"Yes, mama. Eh, Flora, hurry up." Flora was looking for her slippers. We took cover under the ping-pong table in the living room and stayed quiet until the siren signaled that it was safe to be out and about. My parents felt that if the house got hit and the bricks started to fall, at least we had some support over our head. We did find some bombshell fragments in the courtyard, but thank goodness, we survived the three torturous months of bombing. Nonetheless, the Allied Forces did more physical damage to the city than the Japanese.

The World Comes to Alameda

In August 1945 the Japan government surrendered and thus ended the Second World War in the Pacific. My father was anxious to send for my oldest sister, Joan, and my young uncle, my father's half-brother, from where they were boarding in interior China with some relatives while going to school for the past few years. He sent messages and money to them. Things were chaotic right after the war; it was hard to get messages through. Then the monetary systems collapsed and the Japanese currency issued during the war became worthless. The Chinese currency was devalued so much that we had to use tens and thousands of dollars to buy a pound of rice, just like using the old Italian liras. People came back to town to find their homes bombed or taken over by squatters. For some, life was more miserable after than during the war. Thefts and robberies were rampant.

In fall 1945 I was six. Fila finally went to school next door, which left Flora and me at home. By then, my little brother, Ronald, had come along, and Ah Samm had to babysit him. Mother decided that I shouldn't be too idle. One day she said to me, "*Ah Chut,* (my nickname) you are a big girl now. You can help Ah Samm—see what you can do."

I was always obedient. I went along when Ah Samm had to wash diapers and she asked me to help her with wringing the diapers, which I did. (I am sure that she had to wring them again). I followed her when she went up to the rooftop patio to hang the diapers. One day, she said to me, "I have to run downstairs for a little while. You can try hanging the diapers. I will be back."

"Okay," I said with confidence. While I was trying to untangle the diapers, I saw a big fat rat, the size of a squirrel, running around. I was so scared and ran down to my mother crying, "Mama, Mama, there is a big rat up there. I don't want to go up to the roof." And

I refused to go back again. After a while, I forgot about the rat, and went back to the roof with Ah Samm. One day I went up there before Ah Samm and I saw a man removing clothes from the lines on the rooftop next to our house. He stared at me and he looked like a thief; I was frightened but I held back my tears. I ran down the stairs as fast as I could, and I cried, "Mama, *yau chark ah! Yau chark ah!* There is a thief. I'm scared." Ah Samm ran upstairs. By then the man had already gone and so were our neighbor's clothes.

After the war, the British came back to Hong Kong. My father went back home to restart his business and find a place for us. He kept sending messages to find out when my eldest sister and my uncle would come back. But the attempts seemed to fall short; we didn't have any news. Then one night, we heard a lot of commotion out in the street and then knocking on the door. Lora went to check it out. She opened the peephole but didn't recognize the girl at the door. "Who are you looking for?" She asked.

"I am looking for Leung Sui Jung. I am his daughter."

Lora said to herself, "My father's daughters are all here. Who is this girl?" She wouldn't open the door; then she asked, "Who are you?"

"I am Joan Leung."

Lora pondered for a moment, and all of a sudden, she remembered that she had an older sister who had been in interior China for the past several years. Perhaps that was my big sister at the door! She opened the door. For a minute, Joan and Lora looked at each other; however, neither could tell who the other person was. It had been so long since the separation and they had changed. Joan was tired and frightened. Finally, they broke down and embraced each other, crying, laughing, and jumping with joy. They were just teenagers.

That was a bittersweet reunion. By the time my young uncle came back with Joan, he was very sick with tuberculosis. He had had no medical care while he was in Quilin during the war, and the journey back home was long and rough. My father was saddened. He sent my uncle to Hong Kong, but he died in the hospital shortly afterward. He was only eighteen, and I never got to know him. In the summer of 1946, we moved back to Hong Kong and were all together again.

This was the only time I ever lived in China, but I have fond memories of those carefree days in the "big" house during the war. Flora went back to Guangzhou in the mid-1970s when the Bamboo Curtain was finally lifted. She went to the street, *Yil Wah Dai Guy,* where we had lived, to find the house. (Yil Wah Big Street, in reality, is an alley by today's standard). The house was still there; but it wasn't as big as she remembered.

In late 2000, my husband and I went to Guangzhou to visit his siblings and to find the house. We were able to find the street, but the 'big" house was no longer there. The primary school had been converted to apartments. One consolation is that the local government had finally recognized the value of preservation. The street where we lived has now been designated as a historical site, and the traditional Chinese-style homes are no longer allowed to be torn down. As I looked at those old houses on that street, I could visualize my sister and me climbing on the wooden gate in the "big" house.

INTERSTATE 80: EAST TO WEST

Mary-Jo P. Knight

My earliest memory in life is sitting on "Uncle" Dan's lap in my parents' kitchen in Woodhaven, New York City. This was in 1954. I was a happy child with a winning smile. Our house was a semi-attached small three-bedroom in Queens, less than a mile from the Brooklyn borderline and, oddly, surrounded by cemeteries. There were over a hundred children on our block, mostly of varied European backgrounds, with one Jewish family two doors down. My mom stayed home while we went to the local parochial school; my dad was a truck mechanic at a Sealtest dairy farm, working the night shift for extra pay. We shopped for food on Friday nights after Dad got paid. There was always a package of moon pies in the A&P shopping cart for us. Dinner was pizza for the children and Chinese takeout for Mom and Dad.

My parents, myself, my older sister Ellen, and Tommy, my younger brother, traveled by car every spring, either to Maine to see my mom's family and friends or to Miami to see Dad's family. Sometimes we just went to the Poconos in Pennsylvania. Life was pretty good with huge snowbanks to play on and summers at Rockaway Beach, jumping the waves in the Atlantic Ocean. We were the only family on the block to take a vacation away from home every year.

We didn't know that we were not wealthy nor that we were poor. But over time, I began to realize that Mom struggled with making ends meet. Dad and she had made a bargain when they married that he would pay the mortgage and she would pay the other bills on the 50 percent split they'd agreed to. She never anticipated that inflation would eat away her spending power, but not so with the fixed rate mortgage.

Eventually, there were five of us, another sister and brother, Carol and Mike. It was more crowded at the dinner table; bedrooms got shuffled around, until Ellen and I eventually slept in the dining room, which was converted to a temporary bedroom. My mother set the standard on the planet for what "normal" was. The boundaries were strict, as were our manners, speech, schoolwork, chores, etc.

Sometimes I wonder why I was the only one who was sent to kindergarten; I never learned if I was a handful or that, because Tommy was born so close to me, it was a burden-sharing decision for Mom. But I loved it! We sang, painted, listened to reading, and had a wonderful time. When I went to the Catholic school for first grade, I was sent home every day for talking in class, with a Black Star for bad behavior. Eventually I stopped talking, stopped asking questions, and was successfully closed down for many years. But I was a smart child and progressed nicely despite this suppressive atmosphere. How different life might have been, but I don't resent the discipline, the excellent education I received, or how life unfolded for me.

One teenage epiphany was that I would never be dependent on a man for my security. I also never wanted to be a secretary . . . ever!

When I finished high school, I was in the National Honor Society, graduated with honors and a scholarship to SUNY at New Paltz. I was going to be an artist! Then I met my boyfriend and, later, first husband. One of my early poor decisions in life was to pass up the scholarship and skip college. I can't believe my parents actually allowed this to happen, but they were not highly educated and most young girls got married and had babies early in life. So maybe it was not so unusual after all.

I was out of school in June 1968 with no plans. Mom soon announced that July 5th was my day to find a job. I had no idea how to do this! Fortunately, one of my girlfriends had a temporary job on Wall Street and got me an interview. I was working the following Monday as a secretary! White gloves, pink frilly dress, pumps: a perfect young lady entering corporate America.

It was pretty good, however. People were kind to me, taught me what they expected, and I caught on quickly. In a very short time I was working for two gentlemen in the workers' compensation department who took an interest in me and elevated me to an assistant. Within a month, a young, very pushy man was hired and took my job, pushing me back down to secretary. It was very depressing.

After two more jobs, I ended up at a secondary-mortgage brokerage firm of about twenty people. As a secretary in the early 1970s, there was much to learn and several people interested or happy enough to teach an eager and curious young woman everything about this business. This was a "white-shoe" firm. The partners only hired people like themselves, and only after extensive interviews with the candidate and his wife, just to be sure they would fit in. Since I was just a secretary, I never had this extensive screening. In retrospect, it is similar to being a maid. You're fine if you just do your job.

Well, this was now the early 70s and women weren't any longer "just doing their jobs." Women's Liberation took hold: the divorce rate soared to 50 percent and I was right in the midst of the movement. I had also just married my sweetheart, and we'd agreed that he would quit his job and go to college while I worked. I would go at night until he finished up, then I would quit my job and complete my degree. Things didn't quite work out that way.

My boss, Cecil Akre, was the second largest partner in the firm, and one hot, lazy August afternoon, he spun around in his chair and asked me what I was doing. My slightly aggressive answer was, "I am on the phone with my husband with nothing else to do. You're my boss and it's your job to give me something to do!" So he took a few pages out of his client contact book and handed them to me saying, "Call them. See if they need to buy any mortgages."

My life changed that day. I called them, and a bank in South Dakota did indeed need to buy $250,000, and my career was launched. I never looked back. He gave me more to call and I became successful at negotiating the sale of packages of mortgages. I'd been listening for several years to how this worked, and it was respectable work. Some banks needed to raise money to lend to homeowners who were buying homes and some needed to buy mortgages to keep their savings and loan association charters in parts of the country where no one was buying homes. They needed to keep a high percentage of assets in mortgages, so they bought them in Florida, Texas, California, and New York.

Merrill Lynch Capital Markets bought our little firm in 1979 and I became an assistant vice president in 1981. There was so much excitement in this growing field of finance, and I was on the leading edge of it in a great firm. I remember around this time, a potential client I called remarked that I did not have a New York accent; I slowed down my speaking voice so much so that they could actually understand what I was saying!

In 1980 my husband and I bought a small house on the northern coast of Maine with the money I got out of our company sale, an unexpected bonus! We thought we were going to live up there, à la *Mother Jones* magazine, doing all the hippie things that we cherished. He would work and I would have children. But he never got a job, and I was terrified of being stranded with several children and no real financial means to thrive. Mom typed thousands of envelopes on a manual Royal typewriter for extra money when we were growing up, $5.00 per 1,000 envelopes. When my husband remarked, "I can always work in Woolworth's," that was the beginning of the end of our marriage. My career was taking off, and he never did get a job until his father forced him out of his house several months after we split up.

Onward with the Wall Street career, I flew over the Rocky Mountains to attend a conference in Las Vegas, my first time out West, went to conventions in D.C. and Florida, visited clients in Iowa, Texas, Florida, New Jersey, Maine, Connecticut, and Nebraska. There are funny stories, part of being naïve as well as being, what Cecil jokingly called me, "a pushy broad." He was by far the most supportive mentor I ever had in business. He really valued my entrepreneurship, courage, and assistance.

One day while he was away on a business trip, having left instructions to sit at his desk and only handle our clients, one of the other very tall and somewhat intimidating partners came and towered over me saying, "Don't you know you are taking away a man's job?" He was very threatening, maybe even threatened. After all, I was now doing the same thing that the other partners in the firm did, finding clients and successfully closing deals. I sweetly smiled up at him and made an obscene gesture. I was a bit arrogant then, encouraged by the women's movement! He literally spun on his heel, turned, and walked away in a huff. He never said another word about it.

There was another memorable moment when I sat behind the desk of a junior partner, whom I liked very much. He wasn't more than seven years older than me. Every day, while on the phone, he would reach his arm around holding his coffee cup, place it on my desk, and turn back to his desk. That was my signal to get up and fetch him another cup of coffee, which I did for years. But one day I'd had enough. I put the empty cup back on his desk and said, "When you get me coffee, I'll gladly get you coffee too." He simply agreed to this new arrangement, and I felt I had won his respect. It was never an issue again. He got it, in more ways than one.

These battles are still going on today, although the stakes are higher, i.e., equal pay, freedom from sexual harassment, and senior positions for women. I solved my own equal pay issue by working on commission. I was paid for what I produced. I never had to ask for a raise or be submissive to someone for whom I had no respect. The experience I gained by listening, learning, and finally being able to do business with clients that I found myself enabled me to stand on my own two feet and build a career.

By 1983, I was promoted to vice president at Merrill Lynch. In 1985 I was recruited to Security Pacific Capital Markets to set up a mortgage division. I was thirty-four, still pretty naïve about business, but I landed a generous contract, lived between LA and New York City, hired people I knew and trusted and others I felt good about. At the time, mortgage rates were around 11 percent in an oil-sensitive economy. Our team hit another terrible snag when the stock market crashed in 1987. With it, many people were in debt over their heads and few were buying houses, thus, few mortgages.

A new manager came in with two of his best buddies to start a securities trading desk in our division. I slowly faded into the sunset as they spent multimillions building systems. Our negotiated deals took too long, and MBS were the way to make real money (pre-2008 MBS crash!) Unfortunately, one of their traders cornered the market in a security no one wanted, which forced the bank out of business, and it merged with Bank of America. (Same as Merrill Lynch in 2008!)

I remember looking in the mirror one morning in 1988 and not liking who was looking back. I was being asked to do deals that no longer coincided with my values. I was "downsized" in 1989. I remember going to Saks Fifth Avenue that day to buy myself two beautiful summer dresses! Ha! I'll never forget how good that felt.

It took a long time to lick my wounds and find something else suitable to do.

Since 1985 I've sung with a chorus, the Oratorio Society of New York. We met Thursday evenings to rehearse mostly sacred music for three annual concerts in Carnegie Hall. The concert hall was built in 1873 for the Society and we love our history. We have sung Handel's *Messiah* every year since it opened, plus Mozart, Verdi, Faure, Brahms, and most of the choral repertoire.

Some of us traveled every summer to sing abroad. We paid our own way and sang in cathedrals, churches, concert halls all over Europe, China, South and Latin America. We had wonderful times. After five years, I ended up coordinating these summer trips with the tour operators and members. I was able to travel free as part of the package. I spent thirty years singing, traveling, and sharing meals and laughter while having wonderful friends. I served on the board of directors for twenty-five years and am now a director emeritus forming an alumni association.

In 1989 I married an NYC lawyer I'd met in a personal effectiveness training. It seemed to be the right thing at the time. We lived in a small rent-stabilized apartment on Park Avenue and 35th Street. With a new owner, we were moved into a fully renovated two-bedroom apartment, mostly because he gave so much grief to the former owners and they didn't want to mess with him. It was a beautiful place to live, and I loved saying I lived on Park Avenue. What a life!

But I realized that attachments to glitz can be a smokescreen for what's going on beneath the surface. This was a very angry man. I should have realized before we married, when he dumped a bucket of hot water down on the workmen who were disturbing his peace, that this was not going to be an easy relationship. It never stopped. He kicked cabs if they got to close to him crossing a street, mocked me to friends and family when we gathered and grumbled every day. Eventually, friends uninvited us to events ("Oh, you can come, but not him!"). After we ended our sixteen-year disaster, I asked my friends why they didn't tell me not to marry him, they all rousingly said, "We did!"

When I finally found my new career, it was a win-win-win situation, good for my clients, the company, and myself. I didn't want to leave finance; by now it was in my blood. I decided I could be helpful to people who didn't understand how money worked and generally how to set up their own personal financial lives. I trained to be a financial planner and loved it for the rest of my career!

In 2000 I partnered with a client who had lost his big Wall Street job and couldn't replace it. We'd met in 1997 when I did his family's financial planning, and I kept his assets intact through the crash of 2000. He really respected me for this. He wanted to be conservative, and I forced him to stay in conservative investments even though everyone else was buying as many dot.com stocks as they could. He had a family to feed, a mortgage, and two children to put through college.

Together for fifteen years, we built a clientele that shared our values and valued our services. When I left New York in 2015, he bought my half of our business. Our relationships ran deep. We'd gotten clients through the 2008 market crash, helped them pay for college, build nest eggs, and retire successfully.

My mother had struggled raising the five of us, and it left a bad taste in my mouth. She gave up college, begged or cajoled dad into giving her extra money when she really needed it for food, spent her days cooking, doing laundry, cleaning the house, and staying up until the wee hours typing envelopes. I was never driven to have children. It just didn't make sense to me to repeat that behavior.

My partner, Mike Parish, and I made a joint decision in 2013 to move to the West Coast to be closer to his son and grandchildren. I wanted to live outside the seventy miles I'd spent my entire life, mostly in NYC, simply to make a big change. And, I hate being cold! Someone said to me recently that if I wanted to be in snow, just go up to Lake Tahoe. My quick reply was, "If I never see snow again, it will be just fine!"

We landed in San Francisco on Halloween night, 2015, to begin our search for a new home. We'd loved Alameda when looking around during previous visits. The local stores on Park and Webster Streets made it feel quaint; people seemed happy and cheerful. The architecture is beautiful, and I love being close to water.

We had a rude awakening looking for an affordable house, so we decided not to overextend ourselves and bought a two-bedroom condo.

Though I still do business with clients in New York and here, my focus has turned to new friends, singing with Oakland Symphony

Chorus, golfing, swimming (one hundred miles for 2017), but especially to Mike and his family. "My" two young granddaughters are beautiful and I couldn't be happier. They laugh, are huggable, curious, intelligent, and a pleasure to have in our lives.

We are grateful for having landed in such a beautiful place. I have truly been blessed with a wonderful life of travel, music, health, good friends, good family, and a home in this beautiful island city.

My Life in America

Henry Long

In October 1966 my family, which consisted of my father, my stepmother, my sister, and I, boarded a Pan Am airplane departing from Hong Kong for the United States of America. Back then being able to immigrate to America was considered tremendously fortunate because America represented freedom, progress, and wealth in most people's minds, particularly in Asia. The aftermath of World War II and the Maoist revolutionary war that followed it had created devastating hardship and poverty in China and Hong Kong. My father, who had been a merchant, lost his family's business and suffered persecution and internment, and my mother had had to take my sister and me to her family in Hong Kong, where she died not long after. So, like many Chinese in the early sixties, my father was delighted to find out he could immigrate to the United States with his family. At the naive age of sixteen, I was excited to go to America mainly because I would be able to experience firsthand things I learned from watching years of Hollywood movies.

After more than fourteen hours of a grueling flight across the Pacific Ocean and Hawaiian Islands, our plane finally arrived at San Francisco International Airport. It was midnight when we landed. As we headed north along the Bayshore Freeway toward Chinatown in San Francisco, the first thing that caught my eye were the huge illuminated billboards along the freeway. Hong Kong, a small island, did not need or have a freeway to cross town in the sixties, and no such billboards existed there then. When asked what impressed me the most when I arrived in America, I always responded, "The huge commercial billboards." Come to think of it, it was not a bad answer. The billboards were true to the American spirit: free capitalist enterprise, the American way.

In the following weeks after our arrival we tried to settle in Uncle Cheung's tiny apartment in Chinatown. Uncle Cheung was the fourth brother on my father's side. He had come to the United States in the fifties and became a naturalized citizen. Soon afterward he began sponsoring relatives and friends coming to America. It was said that Uncle Cheung had sponsored no less than forty people. He was a strong believer in family reunification. He was well respected by family and friends due to his sincere, kind, and caring nature.

As soon as my family got settled in Uncle Cheung's apartment, however, my father realized we needed to move out because, despite Uncle Cheung's small family, just him, his wife, and teenage daughter, his apartment was too small for two families. Soon my father found a small bungalow in North Beach, and that became my home for the next seven years until I moved out to live on my own.

My father felt that coming to America would give my sister and me a better chance of receiving higher education. College in Hong Kong was extremely expensive and there were only a few schools, so it was very competitive. My father's hopes proved to be well-founded, and I was accepted at San Francisco State University, which I attended for both my undergraduate and graduate education.

During my third year of college, a job at a medium-size super-market was arranged for me with help from Uncle Cheung. The market was in Linda Mar in Pacifica, a long commute by bus, but the pay was not bad, a union rate. I was grateful to my uncle, par-ticularly when I received my first paycheck. From then on I worked hard, attending school on the weekdays and working at the super-market on weekends and holidays. I held that job for seven years, until I graduated from San Francisco State with a master's degree in psychology. Then I found work as a clerk in the social security office.

I remember my father once asking me, "What kind of job can you get with a psychology degree?" To be honest, to this day I don't have a clue. For the next several years I changed jobs often, trying to fulfill the unnamed ambition I had spent seven long years in higher education training for. I was a high school coun-selor, a substance abuse counselor, a resettlement coordinator for Southeast Asian refugees, a marriage counselor, a field researcher in gerontology, and finally a case manager for the developmentally disabled. I considered those years challenging, exhausting, heart-wrenching, and enlightening.

Eventually I landed at the Regional Center of the East Bay in the case management division. My job there was to advocate for and help my clients receive proper health care, living arrange-ments, education, employment, habilitation, and mental health care. I held that position for twenty-five years until I retired in October 2016. I truly enjoyed my work because, aside from my clients' genuine good natures, the job gave me the opportunity to do what I have always believed in, that in the helping professions you have to treat the client as a whole person. You have to take into consideration all aspects of a client's life, including the person's belief system and cultural, educational, and financial background, as well as medical and mental status. The holistic approach is the way to go, and my work allowed me to practice this.

My life might have taken a different turn when I was thirteen. Born and raised in China, my father was not a Christian. He knew very little about Catholicism, but he had wanted the best education for me, and with us living in Hong Kong, he thought parochial school was what I needed. So beginning in the first grade, I attended the Salesian Catholic School–English Division in Hong Kong, where I received a Catholic academic education. During those years I met my mentor, Brother John Kwok, from the Salesian order, and I benefited from his academic knowledge as well as from his teaching in morality and Christian ethics. When I turned thirteen I asked my father's permission to join the St. Francis de Sales order, which had founded the Salesian school. I told my father I wanted to help people with their spiritual and mental growth, that that was my calling.

Being a traditional Chinese man, my father strongly objected to the idea. His explanation to me was that I was the only son in the family and I needed to remain at home to carry on the family name. I believed it was because my father was an atheist and did not appreciate the value of any religion. In addition, the civil war in China had hardened his belief in pragmatism, as well as his view of human nature. Nonetheless, my father's views overcame mine and I did not join the Salesian order. Looking back, I have no regrets about following my father's advice. And all these years later, I consider myself to have been faithful to Christian beliefs and helpful to my fellow human beings. I devoted thirty-some years of my life to helping people who were in need. In a way, I have answered my calling.

Christine Rose Lyons as told to Richard Lyons

Alife-size figure of cartoon character Bullwinkle the Moose gaped at me through the viewfinder of my camera. Bullwinkle stood in the corner of the wood-paneled office of Ray Bradbury— the world-famous author—writer of *Fahrenheit 451*, *The Martian Chronicles,* and countless other stories. Ray's office in Hollywood was filled with mementos of his long career. I turned the lens toward Ray as he sat at his desk behind the old black mechanical typewriter upon which he wrote his stories. I focused on his warm smile and pushed the shutter release. The motor drive clicked off a stream of photos. As I held my camera, I remembered how far I had come.

1956: Soldiers at the Border

"Zatrzymac! Nie mozesz tego wziac. To jest zabronione!" (Halt! You cannot take that with you. It is forbidden!) The soldier pointed to my prize possession, my little camera.

"Musisz mi to przekazac. Nie mozesz zabrac tego z Polska." (You must give it to me. You cannot take it from Poland.) I was eleven years old. Mother and I were at the port of Gdansk, Poland, planning to immigrate to Israel. It was freezing cold, the beginning of an

odyssey that took me from my home in war-torn Poland to Italy, Israel, France, England, and then to the United States—New York, Los Angeles, and finally the beautiful island of Alameda.

Mother protested, "*To tylko mala dziewczynka. Nie moze szkodzic.*" (She is just a little girl. She can do no harm.) I was not a threat to the Communist government of Poland. Why could I not take my camera? Mother did not want bring attention to us by protesting too much. The soldiers did not know that she had sewn our few jewels into the hem of her dress. Jewels that she had traded for when she acted as a "go-between" in the Jewish ghetto in Warsaw during the Second World War. We were allowed to take nothing of value out of Poland and only a little money. If Mother had been discovered smuggling jewels she might have been jailed. I had no other family that survived the war. What would have happened to me?

She said to me quietly. "*Daj straznikowi apparat.*" (Give the guard your camera.) I could tell by her tone that this was a command. In tears, I handed the guard my precious camera, and we were allowed to pass to the dock where a ship would take us to Italy, the first step closer to Israel.

Poland after the War

I was born in 1945, at the end of WWII. My family was Mother, Father, and my older sister. Father was Jewish. Mother was half Polish and half Jewish. As a child, Mother had been baptized as a Catholic. The baptismal certificate saved her and Father's lives during the war. Since she could prove that she was a Polish Catholic, they were not forced to move into the Warsaw Ghetto with tens of thousands of other Jews. This allowed her to walk around Warsaw with less threat of arrest. As conditions worsened in the ghetto, Jews tried to survive by selling their possessions. Mother was a trusted go-between for Jews selling their few possessions and Polish Catholics willing to buy them.

I know about the Warsaw Ghetto from reading and from the few stories Mother told me. She rarely talked about it after the war. It was too terrible. I do know that she and Father had a one-room apartment in Warsaw with a hidden closet. Father hid in the closet all day every day. Homes could be searched without warning at any time. Father and Mother were afraid that the Nazis would discover him and send them both to the camps.

At some point Father was discovered and arrested by the Nazis, beaten, and put on a train to Auschwitz or Treblinka. He managed to escape when the train stopped in the countryside. He begged a peasant to hide him and take him to Warsaw. I remember Father after the war. He would take my sister and me on walks and tell us stories that he made up. When he stopped in mid-story, my sister and I would badger him: "What happened next?" Father would laugh and say that he had not made up the next part yet. Unfortunately, the beating he suffered during the war ruined his health, and he died when I was young.

My sister was a few years older than me. She had to study very hard in school, but once she learned something she didn't forget. I was the opposite. I would only study right before a test, and I would do well, but then forget everything I had studied. My dear sister had tuberculosis. After the war, Poland was in ruins. There was extreme poverty, food shortages, and very little medical care. My sister died from TB when I was young.

When I was born, Mother had me baptized. Baptism had saved her life, it might save mine too. The nuns at the Catholic schools I attended were very strict. I didn't like them, but I got a few years of English classes. I love languages and learn quickly. Even though these were basic classes, their foundation helped me when I came to America.

Poland to Israel

In the late 1950s, the Communist Polish government encouraged Jews to leave Poland. Israel was accepting Jews from any country. Mother, seeing no future for herself and her young daughter in Poland, applied to immigrate to Israel. We were allowed to leave with our clothes and a few belongings (but not my camera). We boarded a ship in Gdansk. I don't remember the name of the port in Italy where we first stopped, but I was so excited. After the hardship of our life in Poland, this was an adventure. In a few days we arrived in Israel and were welcomed as immigrants. Since there were thousands of Polish Jews in Israel, language was not a problem. Moreover, Mother knew Yiddish and German. Our months in Israel were a blur of people and activity as we moved from one place to another to live.

Mother met and married my stepfather Abraham in Israel. They decided that conditions in Israel were too difficult and thought they could find a better life elsewhere. I never learned whether they had a specific plan, but soon we were on the move again. Mother, my stepfather and I traveled by ship from Israel to France.

Seeing the American Flag in France

I saw the American Flag in France. In an article about the American Flag that I wrote and published later as an adult, I wrote about my recollections of seeing the flag:

Oh, how clearly I remember that moment when I saw the flag of the United States for the first time in my life. It waved from an embassy building somewhere in France. I was on my way to England and at that time I had no idea that one day I would be able to live in the United States. Something made me stop to look at the flag and my reaction was quite unexpected. It was an emotional moment. Having just arrived from behind the Iron Curtain, from a country that throughout its history has been almost continuously invaded, occupied, and oppressed by one foreign power or another, to me these bold stars and bright stripes represented a sovereign, independent country, the land of freedom.

London to Los Angeles

My family next traveled from France to London. Mother was pregnant. We stayed in London briefly while my stepfather secured passage for us to New York. I don't know how he and Mother accomplished this, but before long, we were taking a ship to New York. My sister Anita was born in New York City. My stepfather had distant family in Los Angeles and soon we were moving again, taking the train across the country to Los Angeles.

Almost a year after leaving Poland, I arrived in Los Angeles. It was sunny with a warm breeze. The streets were lined with palm trees and every little bungalow had a flower garden in front. The streets were wide and there were lots of cars. Everything was spacious. I had never imagined there was any place like Los Angeles.

I had traveled ten thousand miles to get there, leaving my native Poland for Italy to Israel to France to England to New York to Los Angeles. We left with almost nothing, just a widow and a young girl, not knowing where we would wind up. Now we were a family again: Mother, my stepfather, and my baby sister. I don't know why exactly, but I felt I had arrived home in Los Angeles. This was the place I was meant to be. This was where my life began.

I could write an entire book about my experience of life in Los Angeles. Here are a few vignettes.

The Mystic Eye

In the early 1970s I ran a head shop in Hollywood called the Mystic Eye. Many people don't know the term *head shop*. It means a retail store specializing in hippie and counterculture items and cannabis accessories. I sold handmade leather goods, incense, artwork, and colorful clothing. I also stocked hash pipes and stash boxes. I had a black-light room in the back of the store, where people could look at posters and art that glowed under ultraviolet light.

The funny thing about my having a head shop is that I never took drugs and knew nothing about these cannabis accessories. My boyfriend had a head shop in Los Angeles. He thought it was a good idea for me to open one in Hollywood. He set it all up.

My time running a head shop was brief because I soon broke up with my boyfriend. However, his parents became my lifelong friends and helped me in my budding photographic and writing career.

4E and *Famous Monsters of Filmland*

My ex-boyfriend's father was Forest J. Ackerman, shortened to "Forrey" or "4E." Forrey was a genuine Hollywood character, fascinated by movie monsters and science fiction. For many years he published a magazine called *Famous Monsters of Filmland,* which had behind-the-scene stories about various monster movies. He also wrote science fiction stories and was a literary agent for other science fiction writers, including Ray Bradbury, Isaac Asimov, and A. E. Van Vogt. He coined the term *sci-fi.* Forrey introduced me to Ray Bradbury and others.

Forrey's house was called the Ackermansion. It was an old three-story house in the Hollywood hills, filled to the brim with monster props from Hollywood movies. He was tremendously fun.

Memoirs Found in a Bathtub

Forrey acted as my agent when I was engaged to translate the book *Memoirs Found in a Bathtub,* a dystopian novel about life in the future, from Polish into English. It was written by the most famous science fiction writer in Europe, Stanislaw Lem. My translation is still available on Amazon. Forrey also arranged for me to do Polish–English language tapes with A. E. Van Vogt, and do some illustrations of an exotic, buxom space girl for a sci-fi thriller.

The Successful Living Institute

In 1975 I was invited to a party at the Successful Living Institute in Los Angles. The Successful Living Institute grew out of the human potential movement in the 60s and was similar to EST, but not as well-known. I didn't know it at the time, but the purpose of the party was to get new people to sign up for its programs. At the party, I met a young man named Richard Lyons. He too was an unsuspecting guest. Neither of us liked the institute's programs, but we liked each other immediately. We were married a few years after we met and are still together more than forty years later. I guess you could say that the Successful Living Institute was very successful for us.

Photographic Gal and Writer

I loved living in Los Angeles and Hollywood. I worked as a freelance photographer and writer. I photographed actors and models for their portfolios and did editorial photography for newspapers and magazines. I was a contributing editor for the magazine *Writers Digest,* interviewing writers and other creative people, photographing them, and writing articles about them, including Ray Bradbury (I also wrote, photographed, and produced an educational filmstrip about Ray's life called *The Man in the Wonderful Ice Cream Suit*), Michael Crichton, Alan and Marilyn Bergman (composer-lyricists of "The Way We Were"), Chuck Jones (the cartoonist who drew Bugs Bunny) and many, many others.

I even had a poem and short fiction published in *Playgirl* magazine.

North to Berkeley

In the late 70s I moved to Berkeley so my husband Richard could go to law school. Although I missed Los Angeles, I learned to love the Bay Area. I continued my freelance writing and photography and had a variety of jobs. I also developed a new focus on color art photography. I have several series: windsurfing sails, computer boards, and skyscrapers. My work was represented at the Artist Gallery of the

SF Museum of Modern Art for a number of years. I also wrote humor pieces published in the *San Francisco Chronicle* and other newspapers.

Alameda

In 1988 we came to Alameda. I have lived here longer than anywhere else. In Alameda I discovered a community of artists. Although I had known many creative people in Los Angeles, there was no sense of community. In Alameda I was a founding member of Alameda Women Artists (AWA). AWA is now almost twenty-five years old. AWA includes photographers, painters, sculptors, and other women artists, almost all located in Alameda. We would get together monthly and talk about our projects or listen to presentations. AWA always organizes a yearly art show of its members' work. Alameda is truly home.

Retirement

Ros McIntosh

Long ago when I was working full time, teaching college courses at night, bringing up my children, and cooking, cleaning, shopping, and the rest, I gleefully dreamt of retirement: sleeping in, relaxing in a deckchair, enjoying a good book, and eating often and well. Leisure at last.

But it didn't turn out that way. Far from it! I still get up at five in the morning. An annoying habit I acquired over the years—and habits are hard to break. Like most of us, I have oodles of emails to read, delete, and answer, and it may take an hour or two. And then, instead of reclining in my deckchair and reading the news, I decided to write my memories of the Hitler years, hunger, and deprivation. It became a book, and now, several books later, here I am sitting at my computer again eight to ten hours a day. It's amazing how time flies when you're thinking, reminiscing, and creating.

Live, Laugh & Learn was the title of that first book of stories about my life—funny, absurd, and sad stories, but all true. Episodes of the war years, of even greater hardships after the war, of the kindness of Czech occupying soldiers and our bloodcurdling escape from the Russians, of the joy of climbing trees and the taste of my first orange when in my teens, of the glorious concept of a United Europe and the experience of being an au pair for an

English family that five years after the war considered me still the enemy, and then of a year in France, where friends of my parents warmly welcomed me. I was in Bordeaux when I received my parents' telegram: "Come home at once, you've won a scholarship to study in the US." That scholarship constituted a colossal stepping-stone—henceforth, I returned to Europe only for vacations.

I submitted a copy of *Live, Laugh & Learn* to an editor. Barely a week went by when he called and urged me to write another book exclusively about the Hitler years. The Hitler years? They were buried deep within me, to be forgotten, and never ever to be recalled! They were too painful to remember. I mentioned this seemingly absurd and unwanted request to a young German friend. He looked at me and murmured, "This may not be a bad idea. Did you know that everything we learned and were told about Hitler was far from the truth? Researchers are slowly uncovering the truth—a truth that none of us knew. It's truly fascinating. It will surprise you."

He did not exaggerate. The latest documents of Hitler's actual story are mind-boggling. After two years of research I wrote my next book, *The Madman & His Mistress,* shedding buckets of tears in the process.

The madman is Hitler of course. In his early years Hitler had no political ambition—he wanted to be a painter. As a matter of fact, Hitler and his best friend had lived solely from the proceeds of selling Hitler's sketches, primarily of Vienna's well-known buildings. Yet the Vienna Academy of Art turned down Hitler's application for admission, and refused him again when he applied a second time, stating *lack of talent*. It caused Hitler to fly into a rage. Utterly humiliated, he disappeared for several years. Not even his family knew where he was. Filled with hate and turmoil, he lived in the streets of Vienna, slept on park benches, and ate in charity kitchens. He turned to hate speeches, railing against the government, the educated, and the rich.

The mistress of the title is the German people, not Eva Braun—that poor woman was nothing but a convenience to him. He never loved Eva, in spite of her desperate affection for him. Hitler passionately loved Gelly, an attractive young cousin of his, who with her mother moved in with Hitler to run the household for him. Gelly was seventeen, half his age, and was flattered by the attentions of this clever politician.

Their romance began in 1926 and lasted four years, during which time Hitler became a different person. He ignored politics and no longer attended his party's meetings and engagements. He and Gelly spent every moment together, riding in a carriage through the country, attending the opera, and spending much of the party's money. The National Socialist Party, which had chosen Hitler because of his eloquence, lost many of its members, and in a desperate effort to achieve its political goals it had Gelly killed.

The shocking murder of his beloved Gelly hit Hitler hard. He changed into a raving, hate-filled politician who would stop at nothing. He raced from meeting to political meeting, giving highly emotional speeches each and every day. Before long, the National Socialist Party became the strongest party in the country. In 1932 Hindenburg ran for reelection to the presidency of Germany. Being eighty-five years old, he needed the support of Germany's strongest party to stand behind him. Not surprisingly, Hindenburg's advisors and the National Socialists made a deal: Hitler would be named chancellor if Hindenburg won the election.

The rest is history—a meteoric rise for a penniless, uneducated, friendless chap from Austria, to become *Führer* of the German people.

The Madman & His Mistress became a bestseller. Many readers have asked if the stories were really true. They are true and are based on fact. They are vivid reminders that Hitler and Himmler were experts at deception who created their own glorious stories that they impressed upon the German people and spread across the world, carefully hiding the truth.

But enough of that madman.

It's grand to be retired, even though leisure moments are still rare. A lot of volunteer work fills my schedule. And I have written six books since I retired. One is called *In Search of the Good Life.* Expressed in poetical form, it reflects my philosophy about achieving happiness. What gives us happiness? Is it health? Is it friends? Is it wealth that makes us happy? Another of my books is *The ABCs of Staying Young.* It was great fun writing it because I had no idea what the answer would be. After much thought, and going all the way through the alphabet, I liked the answers I came up with.

Amusingly, the most difficult task I've had in recent years was attempting to translate *The Madman & His Mistress* into German, my mother tongue. But language, I discovered, is in constant flux. I was nineteen when I left Germany. During the fifty years since then my German had become old-fashioned, and I needed the help of several German friends to edit my script before it was published.

My latest book is all about condominiums: *Condo Living, the Pros and Cons.* It's been twenty-five years now that I have lived in a condo, and I still love it. Here is an excerpt from the book:

Actually, the idea of living in a condo had never crossed my mind. I wanted my own garden with trees and flowers, and a large lawn where the children and the dog could play. Then one day I found myself on crutches. Since my house and garden had forty-two stairs, I reluctantly and temporarily moved to a condo. That was twenty-three years ago. My foot recovered, but I never moved back to my house. What brought about my preference for living in a condo? It was the ease of condo living that enticed me. No more clambering to the roof to clean out the gutters. No more sanding and repainting the fence. No more plumbing or electrical emergencies. Even my once so coveted possession of a lawn had lost its appeal. The children had grown up and moved away, and our dog had returned to dog-heaven.

Ah, it's grand to be retired.

THREE STAGES OF LIFE

J. Michael Parish

The three stages of life: childhood, adulthood, and "You look good." I generally believe that anyone who meets me and spends time with me tends not to forget me—the Orioles had a relief pitcher named Al Hrabosky whose nicknames were the Mad Hungarian and Stan the Man Unusual, and he's a hero of mine. I moved to Alameda in 2015 with my partner, Mary-Jo Knight, the love of my life, and our beloved cat, Alto, to be closer to my son, who is thirty-five now and has a beautiful Navajo wife and daughters ages seven and nine. They live in Oakland near Lake Merritt. I also have a wonderful daughter who is almost forty and finally found and married the man of her dreams last June. She lives on the Big Island of Hawaii, with a view of Maui from her front yard, and teaches yoga and works on community organizing. She was elected recently to a seat on the Democratic Committee of the island of Hawaii, which is also a county of the state, in the first contested election for those posts in forty years, despite not being a native Hawaiian and having lived there less than five years.

Mary-Jo and I couldn't have been happier to leave behind twenty-one feet of snow piled up in the cul de sac in front of our New Jersey house and a lot of cold weather besides. Now we play golf at least once a week when it's not raining and see the grand-children once a week instead of once a year.

I'm the first in my family to attend college. My Princeton education got me into Yale Law School, which got me into a great job with a distinguished Wall Street law firm for thirty-five years, and provided my kids with wonderful elhi educations and loan-free college while living in one of the world's greatest cities, across from the dinosaurs and blue whales of the American Museum of Natural History—which was also the block where they blow up the balloons Thanksgiving Eve for the Macy's Parade floats.

Through all this has been the centrality of humor and loved ones to a fulfilling life. I've been a *Jeopardy* champion, a prize-winning poet, and have published a number of poems and stories as well as a great deal of legal writing. Three divorces reduced the bank account by vast amounts, but there's still enough left to see me through, and my kids and all my exes consider me generous. My son dropped out of Yale after three years of straight *As* to save the world from global warming; he now heads the largest solar lender in the United States. At one time he was *Rolling Stone's* "Environmental Superhero of the Twenty-First Century" (environmentalism is still an uphill battle in case you haven't tuned in recently). My takeaway from life is and will always be that people are selfish, greedy, and shortsighted, and we willfully disregard anything that we don't like to hear, including most of science. So my prognosis for the human race on this planet is that we will be gone in much less time than most people think. But now I want to share some funny stuff and some stuff from the heart, that maybe will remind you of yourselves (always the most interesting topic anyway) and that perhaps you will share with the people you care most about.

Global Warning, 1986

Ants shoulder their burdens with well-designed anatomies,
embrace their common condition, carry more than their weight,
and pack plenty on plenty into their granaries.
Spiders sit silent and spin, confident of their kill.
Our speed-fevered buccaneer brains might stop to calculate
from these clear survivor stories a better way to chill:
no one coral cell by any stretch of measure matters.
Hogs at the trough slaughter themselves—
the reef is where well-being dwells.

Time

My father asks a pointed question
to demonstrate a mistake I made
and "allow" me to see that
my thought wasn't
well-considered
really was it?
No
air remains
in this dining room
and the food on my plate
looks drenched in sweat the—
the only thing missing is the time
to think of an answer: he can wait forever.

This man sits there, ice eyes shining, bald head
gleaming, fork stitching his mouth. He
owns the time, his heart throbs at a
reptile pulse—my closed throat
coughs out its reply:
No sir, really
but
that wasn't
what I meant to say at all.
Seconds burn like meteors behind
my eyes. Blackboards glaze with words
chalked over each other, and I have to squeeze
all of them through a pinhole tighter than a drop of blood.

First Daughter

At first you will know her as yours only by a vague contrariness
That characterizes everyone else you love, among others you and myself.
You will see in her your marriage—that is there will be more
Of her mother than you thought you had bargained for.
You will find her set of mind, her greed and resolution to rule,
Rival your own. You will also find them less fully veneered, that
Will come later, you will see to it.
You will find in her a new definition of fatigue, reverberant
Of Quantico and if you pursue the thought you will remember
Pocahontas,
That she did everything except what Powhatan asked or required.
You will find—the most difficult thing—that she is someone
Other than you. That will not change.

You will also find—this must not be sentimental—
That you begin to shun telephones, and newspapers, even more
Than you already do, because you will find that there are some
words
On the telephone you will never want to hear
And because you will find so many stories about children
You cannot bear to read but can't blind your eye against.
You will consider another for insurance and understand after that
The words *unique* and *loss*. It will be an occasion when your mind
Will be fully alive without experience or experiment.

You will discover, one of the more precious things, your ignorance
Of the natural world, because it will become
Necessary not any longer to disguise it.
The new leverage on your mother will offset any excess of humility.

You will learn the pain of revenge, as you revenge
By a newly raised standard of truth the previous lies, the ones
You were born to and fed with and live by. You will possibly forgive.

There is a flower by the name of meadowsweet.
I saw it this year for the first time. We picked some.
I regret that—there is not enough of it where we live—
We should have forborne. *Spiraea latifolia,* the book says,
Not to be confused with meadow queen or meadow rue,
Growing in old fields, native to the Southern Appalachians,
The flower I will have planted over me.
You will find, you now have, your meadowsweet—the book says
"The brown fruits, which persist after flowering, are a distinctive
feature."
You will learn persisting.

Night

We were sitting in the window seat in your room, because you
do not like to sleep in your bed but rather as much as possible
in my place with your hands in your mother's hair, though I
prefer another arrangement. So I put the quilt around you and
as many pillows as I could find and even one against the window—
I trust the window guards but don't insist on that from you, and
we were talking. And you said to me, what if I was watching TV and
I went inside the TV because I wanted to be in there, in the show,
what would you do? And I said I would follow you and find you and
you said but you wouldn't have to do that, I would be a cartoon
then and you could get another son and I said no, I have the son
I want. This is him here.

Family Reunion

Late August sun and a thicket of sumac surround
My head and the raspberries I thought I'd found
And engineered my way down from the path to pick
Are gone in a wrangle of briar and the crack of dry stick.
The assembly of noises I'm out here escaping from
Crashes on, but as background, crowd noise, more hum
than drum.

Seeds and shoots from the same stock stretch toward different light
Determined by your birth or what happened one dark night—
But the sun shines today on our bramble of shared blood
And the sighs and smiles as we sit down to share this food
Say we seek not the berries so iridescent as to thread
The needle of your eye from far away with new berryhood
And then disappear, but the fruits so ripe with home, so red
That they drop in your outstretched hand, provided and sped
by the love of our living and our dead.

Song of Thanks

When I told the birds outside at my feeders

That we had a new baby girl

They all said whoa,

Neat

And started a whirl

In midair, a kind of 3D do-si-do

And chirped a hosanna.

The good guys need more leaders

They trilled, and we can't wait to meet

Tohaana.

Coming In

Because the drops of rain make and destroy bubbles in the surface of the flood that inhabits my courtyard in this October deluge I can see movement—the light from the corridor plays with the rain to make a snowflake pinwheel fireworks display more beautiful than instructive in this downpour.

Pushing the plunger against the drain in this eight-by-eight space of sometime sun brings up the past summer's silt and I know my growing of plants will be the insurance company's defense when I get flooded out. There is movement—I search for sympathetic vibrations, for the water, the plunger and the drain to start to shake and stir with each other, and my tired drummer's arm bends to keep the fluid alive until it gets to where I need it to be—the water up to my shins in the courtyard and the block in the drain, the blending of bled earth and fresh water. My hat, my shoes, and the abandoned Sitting Bull sweatshirt I found downstairs in the laundry room near the plunger are all soaked through. I've pushed as much water as I can. Maybe the rain will stop. Paper has its own humidity. Words are a place to be dry.

Gwen Pirack

Age Six

I lived two blocks from Haight School in Alameda. My first-grade teacher was Genevieve Nicholson. Because I was able to spell the word *chimney* I was congratulated by Principal Ralph Cioffi. My sister, Nita, was three years old. When she was born, I stayed in Vallejo with my Aunt Moyne and Uncle Ira. I remember the sky was filled with barrage helium balloons (blimps) during WWII.

At Haight School a new girl, Luanne, arrived. She always wore a bandana. We became a cliquish club with a newsletter. We called ourselves the Bandana Banana Luanna Club. We became friends.

Eighth grade

I acquired pen pal, Judy, from Massachusetts. We grew up together, writing letters (now down to about five a year). When my children were little, Judy's parents and family visited us while staying in San Francisco. In 2003 my husband, Larry, and I visited Judy's daughter Debbie in Pennsylvania, and then traveled with Judy and her husband, Dan, to the state capitol, and to the largest swap meet in the US, in Hershey. We have traveled with them to Alaska, Oregon, Washington, New York, and New Hampshire.

I became a Job's Daughter as a high school freshman. It is an international character-building organization for girls that any girl can join provided she has a relative who belongs to a Masonic Order or Fraternity. We wore robes during meetings at the Masonic Lodge on Alameda Avenue.

Age Sixteen

Alameda High School (AHS) had sororities and fraternities, and membership was by invitation only. It was a big deal to be a member in either Dianas or Deltas. I had a cousin in each club, and was invited to become a Delta. We organized dances for the student body. I remember a basketball game between Dianas and Deltas. (Deltas lost because they had more cheerleaders than players.)

My friend Julie and I were driven to North Lake Tahoe by her father, Pastor Randall of the Congregational Church, because friends told her work was available as maids during the summer. We decided to camp at Tahoe Vista campground. We walked up the hill toward Crystal Bay, Nevada, through Kings Beach, knocking on motel doors for work. (Sometimes we were lucky to get a ride on a free trolley.) We were hired at a lodge overlooking the lake. The employer worked at Cal Neva Club on the spotlight crew. I was able to see Johnny Ray singing his hit "Cry."

Before work I would have a graham cracker with butter, walk down steep steps to get an inner tube, and float on Crystal Bay a while. At the end of a month, we met some University of California guys who had a red MG. They gave us a ride home. A take-home paycheck of $150.00 was sent to us.

I met Marian in a drama class with Mr. Sisler. After obtaining our driver's licenses, we would borrow our parents' cars and drive to Oakland, by the drive-ins Plaza and Hy's. (We would drag race down Telegraph Avenue.)

I met my future husband at Hy's. He had moved from Oakland to start attending AHS in his senior year. Our high school graduation in June 1957 was in the school auditorium, senior dinner at Del Courtney's. The senior ball was in the gym, followed by an all-night trip to Santa Cruz.

My friend Marian and I used to travel up to Lake Tahoe in her red Austin-Healey Sprite, and celebrated her twenty-first birthday there. She then lived and worked in San Francisco, married, had three sons and last lived in Sunnyvale, before her death.

I took four years of Spanish in high school and joined the Spanish club, but I didn't like tortillas yet. Spanish would be my main educational focus, until I signed up for Spanish literature at the University of California—it was hard, so I switched to French and scored high. I attended college for one and a half years as a decorative arts major, and was a sales girl for school magazine, *Pelican.*

I then enrolled in the Oakland Art Institute to pursue commercial art for one year, and created an art portfolio to take to interviews at various stores in downtown Oakland. I was hired at Jackson Furniture Company and worked in advertising four years before being laid off. I married Larry Pirack at age twenty-one in Carmel.

Age Twenty-Six

I was now the proud mother of Michael (1961) and Paula (1966). Larry was employed at Printing Plates Company. Both of us worked in Oakland, and we would drive to Lake Merritt on our lunch hour. I then worked at J. C. Penney, and did freelance artwork at Travalini, in Richmond. Lachman Brother's Furniture was a new venture for me as a copywriter. The location was 16th and Mission Streets in San Francisco, now the site of a BART station. I worked two days a week and left Paula with Annette, a mom whose son Matt was in Mike's second-grade class.

When I was twenty-nine I was invited to Bible Study Fellowship held at Christian Reformed Church. We studied the book of Genesis. I became the treasurer for one year and a discussion leader for three years. A woman named Sue Garland, who had moved to Alameda from Los Angeles, shared my sandwich at the first meeting. She became my lifelong friend. She was very encouraging to me when we learned that our son Mike had an unknown illness, involving his ability to walk, when he was in fifth grade. Doctors had eliminated cerebral palsy as a diagnosis, and Mike went through months of therapy in a hot tub at an Easter Seals facility and was wearing leg braces to stretch his heel cords, when a biopsy at Children's Hospital revealed that at age ten he had muscular dystrophy, which affects the central nervous system and limits mobility as well as life expectancy past age twenty.

Mike was given one of the first individualized education program (IEP) evaluations at Alameda Wood School and ended up at Porter School for special ed classes, until that school burned down. He then attended Alameda Christian, followed by Montclair in Oakland, and graduated from Concordia High School.

Age Thirty-Six

In the summer Paula and Mike took swimming lessons at the free kindergarten swim program and at Encinal High. Paula was interested in competing, so we joined the Alameda Swim Club, and she swam there and at AHS competitively for ten years. During that time, one of the parents at the swim club took his daughter to Cody, Wyoming, to compete. He liked everything about the area, so he arranged a swim meet and trip there for the Alameda team. Families attended with two busloads of swimmers from Alameda. Our team won the meet and enjoyed river rafting, a rodeo, and a ride to Yellowstone to see bubbling paint pots.

Both children were members of Cub Scouts, Webelos, Brownies, and Girl Scouts. I was a leader (den mother). We had Cub and Brownie meetings in our basement on Pearl Street. Both groups contributed to citywide activities: storefront displays, beach cleanup, and food collection.

Disneyland had been Mike's first trip when he was three. When Paula was three, we returned. Paula confronted a Mickey Mouse, saying, "I didn't know you could talk," to which the costumed Mickey replied, "I didn't know you could talk either." We visited Knott's Berry Farm and my Aunt Merle and Uncle Benny. The kids stayed with them while Larry and I went to Hollywood Bowl for a concert.

Larry changed jobs, and then worked at Good Chevrolet for thirty-four years. I became a teacher's aide for half days at Franklin, Mastick, and Washington Schools. This inspired me to finish my education, and an interview at Cal State Hayward directed me to get an AA from Laney College and then transfer to Cal State for two more years, where I graduated in 1984 in liberal studies and art. Paula also graduated from Alameda High School that year. I was the first person in my family and Larry's to graduate from college. I became a long-term substitute in the San Lorenzo school district, at Washington Manor, for a seventh/eighth–grade split classroom and assisted a track team after school, along with a fourth-grade class studying California missions. I was then hired full time as a third-grade teacher there for eleven years.

Age Forty-Six

When Larry had completed twenty-five years at Good Chevrolet, it was company policy to reward an employee with a trip, usually to Mexico or Hawaii. I had the idea to have him use his gift check toward his airfare to his father's birthplace, Makarska, Yugoslavia. In 1988, Paula and fiancé Michael Dulle traveled with us. A second cousin, Sinisa Zarnic, picked us up from the airport in Split. We stayed with the Pirak family: Katica, Ivo, Karmela, and twins Snezana and Matko. We met countless relatives and saw the bed where Larry's late father was born. (His father died ten days after we were married, in 1960.) Larry's father had immigrated to the USA with an uncle in 1917. At Ellis Island, the spelling of his last name was altered to Pirack, not Pirak, which all the relatives use. Larry's father met his future wife at a Slovenian gathering in San Francisco. They moved to Oakland, where their two sons were born. He never returned home, so he never met his numerous sisters, born after he left.

From Makarska we took a Diesel train overnight to Salzburg, Austria, and stayed there a week in the Hinterthal Alps, with a side trip to Munich.

We have been to Croatia, after Yugoslavia was dispersed into separate countries, a total of five times, and have been to Greece, Italy and Sicily, Slovenia, and Sarajevo, Bosnia. We have visited Korcula, Brac, and the Hvar Islands. I have sent birthday cards every year since 1988 to the cousins, aunts, children, and grandchildren. We keep in touch by email.

Age Fifty-Six

I learned how to make a Chinese paper dragon for the school's Chinese New Year parade. The teacher I replaced showed us directions, and I photographed each stage of the preparation. I have five marching parades on videotape—once we had a baby dragon in a stroller, along with ribbon dancers and a boy waving a stick with lettuce on the end of it, to anger the dragon.

I wanted to host an after-school Spanish club. I went to the National Hispanic University for a master's degree. My thesis was titled, "A Motivational Program for Eight- to Twelve-Year-Old Students of Mexican and Central American Heritage to Reduce School Dropout Rate" (May 1992). My class was required to attend the University of Guadalajara, Mexico, and live with a local family for five weeks, without using English. As the Alameda branch president of the American University of Women, I won both an Eleanor Roosevelt fellowship and PTA California scholarship (1991). I was elated to receive the thrilling news.

The free Spanish club took place during the last five years of the Washington Manor School's existence. The club was for students of Latino backgrounds. We did singing, crafts, Spanish-language practice, and played games. Our annual party had group performances. Sonja, from El Salvador, and Charlotte were my helpers. Parents were often involved, and I trust that those years of participation lingered in the lives of the students. I also taught Spanish at the San Lorenzo evening adult school. Washington Manor School was then converted to a middle school and the staff divided up. I ended up teaching second grade for four years at Dayton School.

Larry and I traveled to Auckland, New Zealand, that year, 1998. We stayed in a timeshare near the home of Sinisa and his wife, Lynette, who had moved back to her birthplace, where employment was more plentiful as the war between Serbia and Croatia limited jobs among the younger citizens. Their twin boys were born there. During our visit, Lynette and I visited Sunnyhills School to compare New Zealand's educational system with California's.

After leaving them, we traveled by bus to Rotorua to see Maori dancing. The next portion of our trip continued to Paraparaumu for an overnight stay at the home of Frances and Maurice Leech. Maurice was my late father's friend and shared his love of stamp collecting. (They lost touch during the war in the 1940s.) He was a retired government employee who had once visited the US on business, when my family first met him. We then traveled to Queenstown, Christchurch, and Dunedin, where Larry and I parted, and I flew to Sydney, Australia, from New Zealand, while Larry returned home to be part of Alameda's 4th of July parade. I wanted to see the setting for the book *Alexander and the Terrible, Horrible, No Good, Very Bad Day*, about a frustrated little boy's desire to move to Australia. I stayed Down Under for two weeks. In Sydney I stayed in a boutique hotel owned by former US residents, and learned how to maneuver by myself. I took a train to Bathurst, home of the Mt. Panorama racetrack, and stayed in a communal residence, where we went horseback riding from Yarrabin.

I took the train back to Sydney to catch a flight to Melbourne, and stayed there a few nights. I traveled to Phillip Island's fairy penguin site, and viewed the Twelve Apostles along the ocean, with their tall limestone spires.

On the Gold Coast I stayed a week at the Mariner Shores resort. I rented a bike, played tennis, attended live shows, and visited Currumbin Bird Sanctuary, where I was photographed holding a koala. Sailing to Stradbroke Island on a tall ship, I met a woman named Lynn, from Victoria. We are still in touch by email. I flew home from Brisbane to San Francisco. A lovely candlelight dinner awaited me.

Age Sixty-Six

I retired from San Lorenzo Unified in 2002 to spend more time with our son, Mike, who was suffering from advanced muscular dystrophy at that time. He was living in a new facility for handicapped people in Pleasant Hill, and going to Diablo Valley College in a wheelchair by van. I often took him to the tennis court, where he had the upper-body strength to return balls with the racket.

My husband and I took a weeklong trip to Palm Desert and came home to find Mike in Eden hospital, in Castro Valley. He was unable to breathe. He had tubes in his mouth and could not talk. We wrote notes for him and he would nod to reply. He had discussed his options with the attending physician and decided that he did not want a ventilator, which was too heavy for his weak chest, or to have to eat pureed food the rest of his life (he loved hamburgers and hot dogs). He chose to be removed from life support and be made comfortable. He died that evening at age forty.

We were very sad to lose Mike. At the funeral, April 13, 2002, Larry spoke to the guests about Mike's desire to succeed, wishfully, as a football player, like his uncle Bob. "Mike did not give up on the battle of life. He won the battle and the score was 40 to 20."

In 2004 I had an opportunity to fly to Perth, Australia, to attend a seminar at the International Federation of Women conference. We contacted Elka, a newly found first cousin on Larry's side, and stayed with her and husband, Mike. We flew there after staying in Goolwa, visiting Kangaroo Island. We reciprocated when they stayed with us Easter week in 2007, with dinner at my sister's and two outdoor parties with friends and relatives.

In April 2008 I went to China on a smarTours trip for nineteen days. I talked my childhood friend Crystal, whose mother had been born in China, into traveling with me. We flew to Shanghai.

It was wonderful to see the gardens and monuments in the city, go to evening shows, and sample Chinese cuisine. We stayed in Beijing and climbed the Great Wall in the rain, not so easy with umbrellas. We toured Tiananmen Square and saw pandas at the zoo. The city was getting ready for the Summer Olympics that year.

Other memorable parts of the trip were traveling down the Yangtze River with sixty other passengers (there was more staff than that), watching the locks at the dam change downstream. We continued down the Shennong Stream in canoe-like boats paddled by men with bamboo poles, then pulled by a rope offshore, coasting on the shallow rapids. We stayed in Guilin and sailed on the river past gorgeous limestone mountains. It wouldn't have been a complete trip without staying in Xian to see the Terra-Cotta Army statues, and three nights in Hong Kong.

Age Seventy-Six

Fifty years of marriage. Larry is volunteer curator at the Naval Air Museum in Alameda, and we used their Crow's Nest for our anniversary party. We had an afternoon party with autumn decor and a seasonal buffet. My brother Jim took photos. Paula and I edited them to publish for a memory book

In 2016 Larry and I embarked on a ten-day tour and flew to Rio de Janeiro, Brazil, where Summer Olympics were held. We visited the massive statue of Christ the Redeemer, on Corcovado Mountain. (It's not scary on top.) We stayed near Iguazu Falls, spectacular from either Brazil or Argentina (it straddles the border between them). We visited Evita's burial grounds and went to San Telmo where we learned how to tango. Adios!

I hope you enjoyed my adventures. One never tires of learning about the rest of the world.

A FEW HIGHLIGHTS FROM MY LIFE

Elizabeth Prosser

When I was growing up in Minnesota in the 1930s, the iceman actually did cometh. A card in your window told him whether ten, twenty-five, or fifty pounds were needed. He would carry a block of ice over his shoulder, holding onto it with big tongs. While he was in the house putting the ice in the icebox, my brother and I would get in the back of his truck, which was filled with sawdust and ice chips, and eat the ice.

The milkman came in a horse-drawn cart. The milk was not homogenized, and the cream at the top was put on our oatmeal. The bottles were glass and you left the empties out to be refilled. We didn't call it recycling.

There was an upright telephone, and when you picked up the receiver that hung on the side, a voice said, "Operator" or "Central" or "Number please," and you said Walnut 3165. Sometimes we would say, "Cherry, I ate one too," (1812) and then we'd hang up and laugh our heads off.

The University of Minnesota cost thirty dollars a quarter then. If you were a tax-paying resident of the state you got in unconditionally.

Cigarettes were fifteen cents a pack. Old Golds were made with apple honey. Lucky Strike Greens went to war. Chesterfields: "Not a cough in a carload." Johnny the bellhop would "Call for Phillip Morris," and then there was "I'd walk a mile for a Camel." The movies made smoking look very glamorous.

My parents used to have couples for dinner and bridge. It was bourbon and water first, then dinner, then bridge. Jewel and Louie Nelson lived across the street. Jewell was from Stillwater, Minnesota, where according to my mother she was top drawer. Melvin and Bea Vogtil. They drank martinis. My father would make a shaker and leave it on the table so they could refill their glasses. One time I sniffed the shaker; it smelled like pinecones. Must've been the juniper berries. I didn't like the taste. How I've changed. Now I drink one every night, sometimes more.

I miss the time when people answered the phone, instead of robots. Telephone booths for calls away from home. Trains with professional waiters in the dining car, the Pullman porters. Those trains were wonderful: the *Empire Builder;* the *Atcheson, Topeka and Santa Fe;* the *Hiawatha;* the *400,* so named because it took four hundred minutes to go from Minneapolis to Chicago. The engineer calling, "All aboard," and then the train whistle. Such luxury and elegance.

In October 1948 my sorority sister Thale Dulebohn and I boarded the *Empire Builder* in Minneapolis for San Francisco. When we got there we stayed at the YWCA on Sutter Street the first night. We had some friends who lived on Post Street. We called and they invited us over. We ordered a cab, went one block and we were there (we didn't have a map). They had two apartments, one for the boys and one for the girls; they invited us to move in. We would share a pull-down bed in the girls' apartment, and cook and eat with the boys in theirs. It wasn't the Ritz.

Thale and I had been assistant buyers at the Dayton Department Store in Minneapolis, so Thale went to work at the Emporium, and because I didn't care for merchandising I became a floor walker at Macy's. The City of Paris was a popular store. They had a notions department where they sold buttons, hairpins, and such. They had someone who mended stocking runs. There was a glove department where you had to be fitted; I wore size seven, long fingers. You bought suede for evening, kid for everyday, white cotton for summer. There was a millenary department; women wore hats then, as did men. There were elevator operators who said, "Call your floor" and "Face the gates."

Rent was $80 a month for a studio on Nob Hill. There was no scarcity of housing. There were guesthouses for single working people, room and board, and the price was right, no one lived on the street. There was the House of Charm, where you learned how to hold a glass of wine, how to sit gracefully into a chair, how to leave a room and close the door behind you. Gracefully, of course.

San Francisco was a different place then. There were no high-rises and Coit Tower was the tallest building in the city. Everything seemed like magic: the Top of the Mark, Ernie's, the Blue Fox—on an alley—the Shadows on Telegraph Hill, where there was sawdust on the floor. The Venetian Room and the Papagayo Room in the Fairmont, and of course Bimbo's, with the girl in the fishbowl. Every night after work we went down the street from our apartment to Elsie's Bar and Café, "Where the smart set meet" (that's what it said on their matchboxes). Elsie, the proprietress, was an ex-madam; Sid was the bartender; and Jinx the waitress. It was a favorite haunt of our friends and it soon became ours. On weekends we went to a North Beach place called the International Settlement. We went to the Bocce Ball for opera; the Gay Nineties for close harmony; the Purple Onion, where we saw Phyllis Diller and Mort Saul; and Lupo's for pizza. We always ended the evening at the Chi Chi Club, where Carroll Davis sang, "Be a clown, be a clown, all the world loves a clown." We never tired of him.

In 1950 I went to work as a social worker for the City and County of San Francisco Department of Public Welfare. I worked there for thirty-seven years and enjoyed every minute of it. In 1969 I met Bill Waterworth. My coworker and friend Anne and I were sitting at the bar in the Domino Club, waiting for our drinks. We were about to light our cigarettes when a hand came around my shoulder and lit them for us. Bill had just moved to the city from Washington, DC. He was working with the navy, and wanted to move to northern California to be near his children, who lived with their mother; he was divorced. We talked for a long time, and then Bill invited Anne and me out to dinner. Anne said she had to go home, I said I didn't. He took me to the Fleur de Lys. A couple of dates later, I learned that the girl downstairs was getting married and moving out of her apartment in our building. I told Bill and he got the apartment. Bill became my life's companion, and until he passed away in 2006.

I believe for every drop of rain that falls a flower grows. Every time I have been fired, evicted, or rejected, it has turned out to be a favor. I always found a better job, better housing, and a better life partner. I sometimes think there's someone up there directing traffic, and that it's all a plot and plan. Several chance encounters (or were they) have changed my life advantageously. One led to a wonderful job, one to the finest housing, and one to interesting times and travel. I was once advised that when insulted or treated badly, instead of reacting in kind, bite your tongue (especially if it's family), the reason being you don't want to feel bad. The result of this practice has been that the perpetrators have rued the day and now treat me like gold and cannot do enough for me.

This stage in life is strange. I used to drive all over San Francisco, making home calls on my clients. Now I drive, but not outside Alameda. When I don't have transportation, I use paratransit, a wonderful service. The drivers are all very professional and skilled. I can't say enough for this wonderful service for seniors and disabled citizens.

I spend a lot of time in a chair, reading and writing. I watch Amy Goodman (a fine journalist) every weekday morning and find out what skullduggery my country is up to. It's usually so bad that I scream at the TV and scare my little dog half to death. Then I rack my brains for something to write for my weekly writing class, take my dog for a walk, work on the crossword puzzle, and confront whatever the day brings. As Bette Davis said, "Old age is no place for sissies." Your arms get weak, your legs get weak, and you can't run as fast. But all in all I don't mind being here.

WAR BRIDE

Trudie Schierenbeck

The letter lay on the dining table, its envelope slit open and the small script visible inside. I had read it once and would read it again after thinking about it. I had to make a momentous decision.

Hundreds of letters had crossed the Atlantic Ocean for three years since my American boyfriend and I had met in my country soon after World War II ended. I had taken a temporary job with the US occupation forces to improve my English.

I was seventeen and hoped to finish my education when the schools were rebuilt after the war. Jerry was a homesick young US army soldier who had fought in the Battle of the Bulge and was waiting for the order to go home. He'd been released from his army unit and assigned to a quartermaster depot in my hometown. His duties entailed driving trucks to pick up supplies for the new post exchange, where I worked. We started talking and exchanged stories about our lives and families. On his last day in Germany he walked me home, and I introduced him to my parents. My mother was quite taken with the polite young man and she understood that there was a spark between us. When we said goodbye, Jerry took off his high school ring and slipped it on my finger. "So you'll remember me," he said, and he promised to write. Two weeks later

I received his first letter from New York. So began our three-year romance by mail.

Now it was November 1948. Jerry's letters became more urgent. Please come over now, he wrote. If you wait any longer you may not be able to come because the War Bride's Act, passed by Congress, is about to expire. Then I would fall under the quota system for immigrants, and it might take years for me to come to the US.

I read the letter again and was torn between my love and my family. Should I follow my heart, or stay with my family? I reasoned that I could always come back to visit. But never see Jerry again? It was unthinkable.

On December 12, 1948, a chartered plane sat on the tarmac at the Frankfurt airport, waiting for takeoff. I was among forty young German brides on the plane. Our first stop was Brussels, where a group of French and Belgian girls came aboard. Next we stopped at Prestwick, Scotland, for British and Scottish brides. All the seats were now filled, and the plane lifted off for the long transatlantic flight to Newfoundland, where we had a last stopover to refuel and time to stretch our legs. The airport there was small; it seemed more like an outpost in an almost barren, icy landscape. We girls walked about in small groups, talking in our native languages. Then we were summoned back to the plane to buckle our seatbelts once more.

During the transatlantic crossing most of us had slept. Now the excitement grew as we took off for the final leg of the flight to New York City. My seatmate and I had already struck up a conversation, and we continued our talk. She told me her fiancé would be flying in from Washington state to meet her, and she worried that his plane would be late. She confided she was a bit nervous about meeting his family. We talked of the sweet sorrow of having to say goodbye to our own families and embark on life in a country unknown to us—but then the anticipation of seeing our sweethearts soon overrode all qualms.

There was lots of chatter. We lined up at the toilets to freshen up. In the lavatory I applied lipstick for the first time. The face in the mirror reflected a red clown mouth—that wasn't me! I wiped off the color because Jerry would never recognize me with blood-red lips.

The plane landed at LaGuardia airport in brilliant sunshine on December 13. Hundreds of people were waiting to see the European war brides on this last chartered flight. I scanned the crowd. Would Jerry recognize me? He knew me as the girl with the French-braided hair; now it was cut to shoulder length. Would I know him, having seen him only in army uniform? A young man walked over to me, wearing a gray topcoat and hat. "Hi Trudie," he said softly, and we just smiled at each other, too choked up to speak.

Jerry picked up my suitcase, took my arm, and steered me toward the exit. "Wait till you see my car," he said, but I only had eyes for him. Six weeks later we were married. We spent a week-long honeymoon in the Adirondacks and then settled into our first home.

Sometimes I think of all the young girls on that long-ago flight and wonder how they fared. Did all of them marry their sweethearts and have a good life? For Jerry and me there was never a doubt.

CHRISTMAS 1945

Miriam Schiffman

My earliest years, in the neighborhood of Dorchester in Boston, Massachusetts, were spent in a world of nighttime darkness. During World War II all buildings on the eastern coast of the US were darkened at night so that enemy bombers would not be able to see what they were flying over. This meant that our window coverings had to be drawn before any light was turned on. During the day I was constantly being warned to be quiet because my father was trying to sleep. He worked the graveyard shift at the Chelsea shipyards. In his forties, with flat feet, he had not been eligible for the armed services. Instead he contributed to the war effort by helping to build destroyers for the navy. When I was old enough to climb out of bed by myself I made sure to be at the breakfast table when he arrived home in the early morning. On occasion I would wake in the night and sneak into the kitchen to sit on his lap while he ate before leaving for work.

Although I was very young, I remember rationing, especially for sugar and butter. My mother would make it a point to count out the ration coupons she had left before we walked the mile or so to the store. I remember saving string and rubber bands and pennies to buy bonds for the war effort. I lived on a street with very large families and we all went to the public health nurse, based in a nearby school, for our booster shots because most of the doctors in the area, including our own family physician, had been drafted. I especially remember being reminded to eat everything on my plate: "Think of the poor starving children overseas." I would not learn how true that statement was until I was a teenager. I remember my oldest cousins in army uniforms, saying goodbye to our grandmother, who lived in the flat above me. They were so handsome I decided I wanted to marry one of them—my cousin Charlie—when I grew up. My cousins fortunately returned safely, and by then my childhood dreams had moved on to becoming a cowgirl and riding my pony alongside Roy Rogers.

What I remember most vividly about that time is the war's end in the fall of 1945. My dad began to work regular daytime hours. Other dads, brothers, and sons on our street came home from overseas. Our family pediatrician returned safe and sound, just in time to tend to an outbreak of mumps on our street. And I especially remember the novelty of seeing lights in our neighbors' windows after dark.

We lived in a mostly Irish Catholic neighborhood. My parents and I, my cousins Carol and Morris and their parents, my Aunt Esther and Uncle Nelson, along with my grandmother, were the only Jewish folk around. We did not celebrate Christmas. However, we were always invited into our neighbors' homes to see their trees and nativity scenes. I found the sight and scent of those beautifully decorated fir trees reaching to the living room ceilings wonderful. My friends would always point out their wrapped gifts waiting to be opened on Christmas Day. I wasn't jealous of them because Hanukah occurred during the same season. We lit candles for eight days, ate special foods like doughnuts and potato pancakes, called latkes, and, best of all, received a shiny new silver dollar from our grandmother.

But Christmas Eve 1945 was special. On December 24th I was allowed to stay up late. I was bundled up against the winter's chill, and when the door to the outside was opened I was led outside to what I still think of as a wonderland: Snow had fallen during the day but had stopped by nightfall, leaving the street, sidewalks, and lawns covered in a white blanket. The stars were shining overhead and the bright moon in a clear sky cast its light on the neighborhood. Everyone else was outside too, slowly wandering up and down the sidewalks. Most of the buildings in the neighborhood were three stories high, with a family flat on each floor, and there were a few scattered single-family homes, all very large. The windows of every house (except ours) were lit up with lights; the trees I had only seen on visits to friends' homes now filled the living room windows with bright color. In some windows candles of different colors were shining; in most homes, from top to bottom, a single lit candle was in each window, some actual candles but most of them electric. All the homes in the neighborhood were lit this way, no longer curtained from the outside world. After five years of nighttime darkness this was truly the end of the war.

Looking Back

Joe Shahpar

A while back I told my grandson David that many moons ago, when I was a teen about his age, a group of us boys—siblings, cousins, cohorts, and sidekicks—spent many idle summers away from our schools and parents, roaming the countryside at my father's century-old adobe compound we called the Red Fort. The fort served as a country lodge for my parents. They loved to go there for its peace and quiet—a quality that was getting scarcer by the day in the big city.

During our summer vacations there, however, our parents remained in town and had no clue as to our activities in the country. They put our fate in the hands of my father's agent at the Red Fort, Hassan Khan, and his wife, Maryam, who ran the fort for my father. They managed the fort staff and about twenty to thirty sharecroppers and their families, all of whom resided in the fort. Hassan Khan and Maryam were to feed us, force us to bathe, make sure we got enough sleep, and if the occasion arose, discipline us. Neither Hassan Khan nor his wife ever laid a hand on us during our stay with them. They had a strikingly beautiful fifteen-year-old daughter, Sara, who was fascinated by us boys running around her domain. She was like a sister to us. We came to like her. Thus, a human connection was established between us boys and Hassan Khan's family, a connection that tended to soften the formal owner-contractor relationship they had with my father. Hassan Khan and Maryam treated us as if we were their own kids.

An unknown person had built the Red Fort in the 1820s—that was the best we could dig up from the yellowed pages of county records. The fort had a rectangular footprint, and its superstructure consisted of six-meter-high periphery walls, seven-meter-high corner towers, and one massive double-panel gate on its south wall, the only access point. The gate, made of hardwood reinforced at the edges by filigreed cast-iron molds, was gigantic and creaked when pushed open, which required at least two strong-armed people. It was closed every night at exactly eight o'clock. Not that, in those early years of the twentieth century, the residents saw any need to defend the fort from an enemy takeover, but in fact there were bandits roaming outside in the dark, trying to steal livestock. A few old-timers believed that nocturnal ghosts tried to get into the fort. Hearing that nonsense made the imaginations of us kids run wild. We also heard that the ghosts loved to steal and devour livestock, and occasionally, humans. In those days the opium-addiction rate was high among the elderly in the fort.

The Red Fort's walls were two meters wide at the base and narrowed to a meter and half at the top. A walkway loop crowned the walls, passing through the towers at the four corners. The fort stood on a low bluff, with a commanding view of the encircling open fields. To me, it looked majestic. I had just finished reading an illustrated Persian translation of Sir Walter Scott's *Quentin Durward*. I couldn't help but imagining our Red Fort being a mud version of Scott's medieval stone castles.

My grandson David suddenly stopped me cold in the middle of my story. He wanted to know how my father, who presumably had been a poor man at the time, had managed to get his hands on a piece of property like that. Good question, I replied. Then I went on to explain in detail the story of the rich old lady . . . My father had been probably just plain lucky, I said. His bastion on the bluff and the many hectares of land that went with it, were a gift from the generous lady. She'd been in love with him. Whether he had been in love with her, I couldn't say with certainty. David said, "I hope someday I'll be as lucky as your father." I wondered whether, if David were female, he would utter a different quip. I went back to my story.

The massive gate on the south wall opened into a hundred-meter-long covered passageway that looked and smelled ancient to me. In that long, arch-roofed corridor, one could see the remnants of an animal feed storage, a horseshoeing shop, a hearth, a wooden water trough, and a row of steel hooks to hold four-legged animals at bay. A dilapidated wooden platform, at one time serving as a resting place for weary travelers, was being used to store wooden pallets. The old passageway had definitely been transformed many times in its long life, but it retained its old aura, and to us boys it looked spooky.

As I mentioned before, I said to David, there was a walkway on top of the fort walls. It provided an all-around commanding view of the encircling open fields, and the view was grand. We climbed to the top of each tower through its narrow circular stairway. It was a dizzying experience. On the top, we gazed out into the open field to spot imaginary enemies, which we differentiated by their shields and coat of arms: Some had crossbows on blue. Some had two gold lions on red—those were the Christians. Then we spotted the Muslims: curved silver swords on black shields. We shot imaginary arrows at them all. We hurled stones at their advancing heads. We dislodged their ladders and prevented their soldiers from reaching the top. In our nearly hallucinogenic excitement we believed the battle scene was real. We were ecstatic. We felt as if we were on some mysterious voyage of discovery. We examined every nook and cranny we came across, looking for things that only existed in our minds. Afterward we sang patriotic songs and swung our swords on our way home.

Only a few times during our stay did we dare to enter the underground network of qanats in our area. Qanats are underground tunnels that collect melted snow from the peaks of the Alborz mountain range north of Tehran and carry it one hundred and fifty kilometers, filtering the water as it moves through the porous earth, to water the rich plains. Standing in the towers we could see in the distance the starkly bluish-white peaks of Alborz reaching out above the thin brownish layer of smog covering the city. A warning sign at the qanat entrance warned us not to enter the system. We did anyway. In total darkness, we relied on our pocket flashlights. We shivered walking in the cold running water that was deep enough to reach our ankles. Suddenly we heard a rumble in the distance. We became scared, turned back and started to run. A couple of us slipped and fell, got up and started running again with the rest of us. The rumbling became more audible. We made it out of the tunnel opening in time. Behind us, a section of earth above the tunnel collapsed. The next day we found out that there had been a mild earthquake . . .

It seemed like I hadn't lost David's attention yet, so I continued. I told him that running around wild in the country made us feel invincible. We had no obligations, I said. We had no cell phones, no computers—they didn't exist—no Facebook, no YouTube. No girlfriends, no Amazon deliveries, no bills, no pressure. Food and lodging were free of charge. When I think back, we had it all.

David laughed, a dry laugh. His innuendos were confrontational. Grandpa, he said, why the hell do you think not having these amenities in your day made your life happier then? Because

I didn't know anything about them, I said, and therefore I didn't miss them. He persisted, But now that you know, why do you think not having them is the way to go? I ignored him. I told him that in the countryside around the fort, we rode donkeys, horses, mules, and the vehicle of our choice, bikes. Hassan Khan was nice enough to provide them to us. We aimed on pedaling as far as we could, and enjoyed dodging agitated goats that ferociously charged at us as if we were Spanish matadors. We helped farmers shear sheep. Under the occasionally intolerable midday heat, blue sky, and burning sun, we climbed trees half-naked to pick fruit for the farmers who had been nice to us. We ended up scratching our dry itching skin to no end. The experience was pure torture, and we felt like heroes.

I told him about my friends' and my transcendental sojourn into the forbidden feminine world. Hearing this, David's eyes opened wide. One evening at the sunset, I said, we climbed a ladder to the roof of the ladies' hammam, their bathhouse. Once on the roof, we crawled to the glass dome at the center to peek into the lit bathing hall. We saw women young and old disrobing and scrubbing their bodies with loufahs. Some were rubbing their thighs, some were feeling their breasts as if unhappy with their size. One of the boys mumbled, Women are vain creatures. The view was enticing. A strange tingling bordering on anxiety overtook me. We all kept silent. We ogled the array of alabaster skin, the pointed breasts of some of the women, their mysterious deltas. We refrained from juvenile commentary. It was a moment of solemn discovery. At that moment, everything seemed genuinely serious to me. By contrast, the women in the hammam were jovial. We couldn't hear their words, but they were giggling and their body language made us believe that they were having a ball. Suddenly we thought we heard somebody climbing our ladder.

We became petrified. What if they caught us red-handed? We fled in a hurry.

Summers are hot and dry in the central plains of the Iranian plateau. For centuries, adobe dwellers of the plains, not having access to air-conditioning, relied on tanurahs for cooling their naturally insulated thick-walled mud houses. Resembling a closed flume built on top of a house, a tanurah is a tall adobe tube that draws in cool air from the higher elevation and delivers it into the dwelling at a lower elevation, creating a cool draft. No electrical usage, no monthly fee, just a gift from nature. Tanurahs operate on the thermodynamic principle that different temperatures and pressures at two different points create a natural flow between them. Hassan Khan's residence in Red Fort had a tanurah, and at the end of a hot day, we boys enjoyed lying down in front of the cool draft in Hassan Khan's living room. Maryam would serve us homemade sekanjabin sherbet, a sugary concoction of spices and boiled mint, poured over ice in tall glasses. Burned by sunshine, exhausted from running around, we looked like a bunch of undernourished Punjabi urchins, and we needed calories and a quiet, cool lie down.

Every night we promised each other to take a bath the next day. We were lucky if we took one every other day. We refused to go to the men's hammam in the village. Instead, we dived in the murky pond next to the giant old mulberry tree behind the north wall of the fort. We'd wash our bodies in its brown brackish water. The pond was home to many other creatures—fishes, crabs, snakes, and larvae. A heavy black goo covered the bottom, and we'd dive down to it, looking for treasures. All we found was discarded junk, but it was fun.

One night in my sleep, I fantasized about Sara, Hassan Khan and Maryam's daughter. I knew that Sara sometimes sneaked behind the mulberry tree and watched us boys diving naked into the brackish water of the pond. Our tanned bodies fascinated her. Hardly anyone ever came around the pond area to see us, so, we were all safely out of sight. We were in our high school years. Our hormones had started acting up. Sara was fifteen. In my sleep, I dreamed that Sara had the hottest pair of legs. She was in her rolled-up loose skirt, walking through mud up to her ankles. I woke up. Reality sank in. None of us boys had ever touched her. After all, we were living in her household, she was like our little sister. Every morning she showed up in her loose, flowery chador to bake our morning bread. After a minute or two, frustrated by the chador, she'd throw it aside and walk around in that short loose skirt, her bare legs showing. When I recalled my dream about her, I was ashamed of myself. Those heavenly tanned legs. I became confused and thought I was having an identity crisis.

I remember our breakfasts at the Red Fort: a steaming polished silver samovar with a large red rose–patterned china teapot of black tea resting on top; feta cheese kept fresh in a bowl of cold water; small bowls of dates and nuts; heaps of fresh fruit. Sara kneaded bread dough between her palms and then smacked the dough against the hot interior wall of the hearth. A while later, the puffed-up bread in all its glory was ready for our consumption.

I had hoped that going over my bucolic past would convince David that being ignorant and having less is a blessing. But it didn't happen that way. During my lengthy sermon, David seemed to be losing his concentration. He became antsy. He nearly said I was talking too much. Meanwhile, he was glued to his phone. As far as I could tell, he was unhappy, reading someone's message on his screen. He mumbled, "Fuck," the four-letter word that is so misused today. The upsetting message David had read on his phone was an email, a text, a tweet, or some other social media vehicle

I was ignorant of. I thought of the many choices we have to deal with these days. I didn't know about a lot of them, yet that lack of knowledge did not bother me. I felt delightfully unburdened. Not knowing everything is living longer. Not being familiar with all the gadgets these kids have at their disposal these days is our way out. To hell with the cyber world.

I was now even more convinced that when I was a kid I had it better than what the young generation does these days. It was sweeter when I didn't have many things and didn't know that I didn't have them. My philosophical views, my comparisons, and my convictions, however, seemed to have no influence over David. I couldn't dent his position. He insisted that I, his dear grandpa, just didn't get it. So far you have entertained me with the dorky picture of life in your teens, he started. I don't believe that depriving yourself of the amenities of my generation has made you any happier in life. Get real, Grandpa. Look at what is being accomplished these days in the market, by private research, by Silicon Valley gurus—There! He had reverted to Silicon Valley. His icon. No use, I told myself. I could never convince him that today's complicated life is the source of today's unhappiness and unrest. Complexity of life was what made David cocky. He believed it made him smarter. Unhappier and sadder, it could also be.

We didn't get anywhere with our back and forth arguments. I was getting flustered. He was getting fed up. Suddenly he looked me in the eye and said, Let's face it Grandpa, your generation just wasn't *civilized*. Ouch!

WELL, AWAY WE GO

Bill Soares

W hat a wonderful life I've had for a man.
I was born in Alameda July 20, 1941, and went to Lincoln School from kindergarten through the eighth grade. They have since torn down that school, which used to be on Central around Court Street. I had my first date at eleven years old. I also had an *Oakland Tribune* paper route then; my route covered Encinal, Versailles, and Central. The Sunday-only paper cost eighty-five cents a month.

I believe I lived a normal childhood for my time. We had no TV until after I finished high school. As a kid I played outside in what is now called Pea's Court, then Pea's Alley. We had a crew of about ten kids and I was the oldest, so I initiated and named most of our games. We used to shoot rubber-band guns at each other—guns we made ourselves. We also played baseball on Broadway between Encinal and San Jose. My family ate dinner at 5:30 every day and we all sat at the table together. Then I'd go outside and play some more until the streetlights came on.

I guess my worst time when I was young was starting at Alameda High School. After only one week in school I got sick and was out for two weeks. Going back, I found I was way behind everyone else and I never did catch up that year. Not only was I behind in learning, I was also the second smallest boy in the school, five foot one and 101 pounds. Sophomore year was better. I met a girl on my paper route and learned how to kiss.

I'm a cheerful guy and have always had a lot of energy, so I finally got in with the cliques at the high school and life was good. I lived on the corner of Broadway and Encinal and had a '50 Ford, so my house became the place to hang out. Other guys would come by and wash their cars on Saturdays. Naturally the girls would come by too. During high school I got my first job, at Bamboo Kitchen at Willow and Lincoln. It's still there. I made a dollar an hour. After high school I attended Oakland City College and lost track of high school friends except for Bill Orr. Bill taught me to smoke and drink and we became good friends all through life.

While going to college I worked at the Regal Gas station on Park Street and Eagle Avenue. Gas ranged from seventeen to thirty cents a gallon. Regal used to give away a Cadillac every month, and customers got a coupon for the drawing when they bought gas. While I was working the graveyard shift one Saturday night, a highway patrolman came into the station and asked for a coupon. I gave him one. He told me he wanted more, and if I didn't give him more it would be bad for me if he caught me on the freeway. Regal ended up stopping the Cadillac raffle because the CHP guys were winning all the cars.

I don't know if you ever heard the expression at home from your parents, "If you don't like it here, you can move out anytime!" My sister was three and a half years older than me and went off to college. Not long after that, I heard the same words and took my cue. I was ready by then, so I made an agreement for a back room behind a beauty salon on San Jose for twenty dollars a month. I even had my own kitchen.

My third car was a '55 T-bird with a stick shift—I had it for about a year. A girl who was a junior at Alameda High took a liking to the car and understood that required her to have a liking for me as well. We had great times together. I'll leave it at that.

Meanwhile, I was doing poorly at college and dropped out. By now I was working full time at Regal Gas. My sister's husband's brother (it is a small town, Alameda) was a year younger than me. He and I followed my sister down to Fort Ord, where her husband was playing "army" for a few weeks in the summer. He bought us a case of Country Club Malt Liquor. We drank, threw up, and got to know each other. His name was Dave and he'd been sent to a military school. He had a good friend in Pittsburgh, Pennsylvania, so we took off in my new Pontiac '60 Tempest, stayed a month with his pal, and drove back here. I went back to Regal and Dave worked at Owens-Illinois Glass Company across the Fruitvale Bridge. When we compared paychecks, I saw that we worked the same hours but he was making a hundred dollars more than I was. So I went to work at Owens.

What an education I got! I had put women on a pedestal, and now I was exposed to the foulest language I ever encountered, and I got goosed many times. I was nineteen and there were a whole bunch of thirty-to-forty-year-old ladies there who thought I was cute. The strangest one was a woman I thought was much older than me, but was actually a year younger. I realize now it was her 44DD bra size that put me off the track. My high school girlfriend didn't have much trouble figuring out what was happening, so that was that with her. On the other hand, Rose, from Owens, was part of my life long after that.

I got laid off at Owens and went to work for a guy who had a shop in back of his house, doing tool and die work for companies. Life always has surprises in store for us, and about two weeks before Christmas 1962 I got two calls. One from the high school ex-girlfriend, who I'd been out of touch with, so to speak, for quite a while. She told me she was pregnant, but it was not mine. A week later, Rose told me she was pretty sure she was pregnant. At Christmas Rose came over, said she was pregnant for sure, and said she was sorry that she'd told me she was taking something to keep from getting pregnant, but that's the way it is.

The day after Christmas I signed up for the draft. In January, Bill Orr and I were playing pool in a bar on 14th, and Rose's stepfather walked in and said Rose and I were going to get married. They had already been to my parents' house. Somehow I talked my way out of that. Then I got a letter to go to court in Hayward on February 13. Rose was taking me to court. I never showed up. I was inducted February 14, 1963, with basic training at Fort Ord and advanced training at Fort Gordon, Georgia. Every graduating class was going to Vietnam, but I lucked out and was one of forty soldiers sent to Germany. The second week over there I walked into the orderly room, and the clerk asked me if I could type. When I said yes, I became his replacement and got a weapon that shot words instead of bullets. How lucky can a guy get!

My sister wrote me to say that her sister-in-law, who was three years older and had a car, was looking for someone to travel with if I behaved myself. I got time off, and she and I drove through Sweden, Denmark, Germany, and Holland. She spoke fluent German, so we got around easily. Later I went to Rome with an army buddy who'd been born there, and to France, Luxembourg, and Salzburg, Austria, when the Winter Olympics were on. I think you must know lots of ladies were part of this happy picture. Meanwhile on the home front, I got two Dear John letters from ladies who were getting married, neither one from Rose or the high school girl. Meanwhile, my mother went to visit the high school girl, who opened the door with a baby in her arms and yelled out, "It's not Bill's." Not long afterward, my mother got a picture from Rose of a little baby, which she sent to me in a letter asking if there were any more "surprises."

I was demobilized at age twenty-three in February 1965. The first thing I did after arriving at home was take off that uniform. My father gave me my Tempest all paid off, which I sold right away. I found my buddy Bill Orr and we went drinking. He said let's go to Reno and offered to lend me a hundred dollars. I won that much and paid him back, and then he borrowed some from me. After two weeks home from the army I visited my godfather, who worked for Canada Dry as a supervisor, and he got me a job in display. After a while I got another job in sales. By then I owned a '64 Plymouth, and my employers put me to work on the Alameda route. That included Lou and Vern Anderson's store, Lou's Liquors, right next to Regal Gas, as it happened. I worked part time for Lou's for eleven years.

At first I lived with my folks for two months. My mother was babysitting for a single mother, and kept saying, "This woman wants to meet you." Finally I met her, "Jane." She told me she was moving into a new place and could I help her. I worked for about six hours and then we took a break and shared some wine. Next thing I knew she'd gone into the bedroom and come back wearing only a see-through nightie. For a while I could drop over any time of day or night and she'd let me in, until one night a guy came to the door. So, again, that was that.

While on my Canada Dry route I ran into a cousin of Rose's at a coffee shop, and he told me Rose was married but unhappy. I called her and we met, and she brought along our three-year-old daughter, Cindy. Meanwhile, Canada Dry had let my godfather go, and when I tried to start up a union shop, they fired me. The union called and told them that was illegal and they had to hire me back. Never happened.

I was now driving a '64 'Vette. The owners of Lou's Liquors wanted more time off, so things worked out, and then they got me a job driving for East Bay Beverages. I stayed active otherwise, if you get my drift, but I started seeing Rose again on the side. A year later she'd gotten a divorce, and at age twenty-five I had a wife and was reunited with my daughter.

One day while I was inside a bar reloading empty beer cases with bottles we recycled, my truck was stolen. I didn't know the plate number of the truck, but it didn't take long for even the Oakland cops to find a truck with Falstaff beer signs all over it, crashed into a fence two blocks away from the bar, and a bum trying to run down the street with a full case of Milwaukee's finest. No charges were pressed.

During my beer-driver days, it seemed like we went on strike every three years when the contract was up—it was the only way. I got to know Herb, the owner of the Hamm's Beer company, while carrying a picket sign, and the next thing I knew I was driving for Hamm's. Rose and I bought a house in Hayward near her old neighbor. We got the place for $21,500, but had to get the seller to carry a second mortgage for $600 because the Corvette wouldn't do anymore in my new situation and I needed to buy a '65 Plymouth Barracuda.

During the next beer strike I got a job, again through Lou and Vern, selling a new brand out of San Francisco called Premium Products. Since I'd done Canada Dry and the beer truck thing, I knew everybody and they knew me, and since the liquor prices were the lowest anywhere in California, pretty soon I had wells in bars all over town. I also got word that another liquor distributor, Young's Market, that had been around somewhat longer needed a new salesman. When that company eventually found out I was the guy from Premium Products who was eating their lunch, they hired me. The owner was the greatest boss I ever had. It didn't hurt that we had the same birthday and he'd been born in the town in Germany where I'd been stationed in the army. He was the first person I ever heard predict that people would start paying good money for bottled water.

Meanwhile, Rose had started dropping hints about wanting to be single again. Everybody— married, live-in, or whatever—needs space. Rose would go out on Friday nights with her best friend, and one night she met her first true love, whose wife had died. I got the house free and clear and low child support when we split up not much later.

My new employer gave me an Alameda sales route. So I rented out the house in Hayward and moved back to Alameda. I was working twenty-one hours a week, 7:00 a.m. to 3:00 p.m. mostly, and owned a '75 Vette and an Olds, hardly had to work at all, and people were buying me lunch and drinks left and right, and taking me out golfing. The Friday sales meetings from 8:00 a.m. to noon, followed by lunch, were the highlight of my week in some ways. I even won a Ford car in a contest. I didn't have the most sales, but the boss said he'd given me the toughest territory. I got married again, and six months later I was divorced.

Another highlight from my life at that time: The symbol of Black Velvet whiskey was the blonde in the black velvet dress, stretched out across billboards all over America. I would set up fifty-cent drink nights at some of my bars, and the blonde, hired by the company, would dress up and come with me. She was always complaining about how she got no attention from her husband. One night the company paid for her to stay at a motel near Jack London Square. I picked her up there and she asked me to zip up the back of her dress, which showed me she had no bra on. We went to work and she did her job, putting Black Velvet stickers on all the men who were drinking it, at fifty cents a drink, along with a hug, while I sat there drinking for free. At the end of the evening she invited me in. When we made our next move she turned to me and said, "Sorry this bed is so hard." I called her beautiful, and we went from there.

I had been bowling for years on Sunday mornings with a group of friends from 8:00 to 10:00 a.m. at Mel's Bowl at the end of Park Street. Over time, the other five guys had become members of the Alameda Elks Lodge, and they asked me to join. Around the corner from where I grew up lived a father figure who'd taught me carpentry and woodworking. I'd even dated his daughter. I told him then that I wanted to be an Elk. He had been what they call a Past Exalted Ruler. I was thirty-two then, and he told me it was time to join, and I was in.

I was immediately installed on the bowling team. At the end of the season, they made me president of the league. People don't realize that most of the things that happened in Alameda in past years were discussed at the Elks at lunchtime. Anybody who was anybody, police chiefs, judges, business owners, were all Elks. The big round table was where business was done. The table that held eight comfortably would have twelve to fifteen people around it. In fact, it was at that table that Mastick Senior Center got going; the men who started it are all named on the plaque in the social hall, and all were Elks.

At thirty-five I went for marriage number three. We bought a house at the corner of Liberty and East Shore. It had to be a corner house because we owned seven cars, all American-made of course, including a Corvette. I worked on various Elks committees over a seven-year period, during which I also quit my liquor sales job—too many rules—and bought a bar in Alameda on Lincoln. I was forty-three then. Partway through the process that marriage died too. I believe it's all that committee work I did that helped me finally get designated an Exalted Ruler—the first unmarried one! That and bowling with the same five guys every Sunday morning for decades. At first we used to go to the Club House Bar on Park St. afterward to drink, then we all went to the Elks. My latest ex made a good profit on the house, so once again, that was that, thirty-two years ago now.

I never gave up bowling or the Elks, but I did get out of the beverage business. I retired January 30, 1997, bought a motor home and traveled for five years, then lived in New Mexico for another seven before returning to Alameda. Now I cochair the thrift shop at Mastick, so come and see me there Tuesdays and Saturdays.

A RADICAL LIFE

Gayle Southworth

I grew up on a farm in South Dakota and was born with a gift for math and logic, which helped me earn PhDs from the University of Wisconsin in math, economics, and history. A lot of what was most important in my life happened during the turbulent era surrounding the Vietnam war, the struggle for civil rights, Nixon's lies and follies, and an enormous campaign of oppression by cruel and cynical despots in Central and South America against the people of those countries that was financed and supported by so-called anti-Communists who ran our government and, even today, continue to do so in a different style, but with the same tax-payer-supplied resources and the same horrific results. Their actions have caused the deaths of thousands of innocent people and the displacement and dispossession of millions.

I got involved because of an organization of Catholic nuns and lay people that tried to help the huge number of refugees from Central America who were leaving Salvador, Guatemala, Honduras, and other countries in that region. Most of these refugees from dictatorships just wanted to live their lives peacefully. There were a few courageous ones, however, who were eager to help us educate the American people about what was being done in our name. We set up a very large-scale speaker's bureau that provided speakers to college and high school classes, churches, and community organizations. We talked to reporters, radio, and TV programs and politicians. This work provided the embryo for what later turned into the Sanctuary Cities movement. The first city council to approve our sanctuary legislation was Berkeley. Oakland, San Jose, Mountain View, San Francisco, and many other cities followed suit.

Another strong memory: At a point in the middle of earning one of my graduate degrees, I found myself as part of a protest group marching against government brutality, the Vietnam War and racism in our own country. A phalanx of riot gear–clad policemen charged our group, which was peacefully marching and chanting the familiar slogans of that time: "What do we want? PEACE! When do we want it? NOW!" "Hell no, we won't go!" "Out now! Out Now!" and singing "We Shall Overcome" when we got tired of shouting. No Violence was our middle name. I watched as these cops chopped down our marchers with their cudgels and used their shields to knock scores of people to the ground. The next thing I knew, a dozen of them grabbed a young black man from our midst, threw him to the ground and started assaulting him with weapons and their boots. Another cordon of police organized to protect them from those who tried to rescue the victim, and then several of the assailants dragged him up and started to haul him away by his shoulders. There was only one difference between this young man and most of our crowd—he was black.

Suddenly, a young woman in a Mother Hubbard dress ran ahead of the cops who were hauling him off and threw herself down in front of their legs and tripped them. I immediately did the same to several of the rest of the cops who were again trying to seal their "brothers" (odd word, right?) off from the marchers. Then I saw a very large young white man wade into the fray from the sidelines, punch a couple of nearby cops, pick up the black guy, and hoist him in a fireman's carry over his shoulder, back through the onlookers and into a black Lincoln Town Car, which sped away.

I was arrested, of course, and beaten and interrogated, but there was no case and they finally let up. Some judge or police sergeant had set my bail and a well-dressed woman came to foot that bail, as the expression goes. She led me out of the jail and toward a black Lincoln Town Car, where I met the large Prince Valiant guy from the protest, who turned out to be her bodyguard. She was an immensely rich heiress from the Fortune 500 list and dedicated, as it turned out, to the same causes I was. So I became a peace and justice activist, and continue to be to this day, with heartbreaking results for anyone who cares about those subjects, or human dignity.

My first college teaching job was at Kansas State. I was to teach the economic history class to freshmen. I began at the beginning, explaining thoroughly that domesticating animals allowed our hunter-gather ancestors to transition to an agricultural economy in permanent communities. If the forests were out of deer, sheep could be butchered. This new form of wealth also allowed the separation of people into classes; some owned wealth, others didn't.

I also added that repeated use of language gave rise to the growth and development of our brains. A larger, more active brain led to the accumulation of knowledge, which, alongside the accumulation of wealth in the form of domesticated animals, led to civilization. Events that at that time could not yet be explained (earthquakes, floods, lightning, plague) were attributed to supernatural beings like Thor, Neptune, Zeus, etc.

After an hour of my talk and plenty of lively questioning I was feeling quite good about my summary, claiming that the three developments with the greatest impact on human development were: domestication of animals, the development of language, and the creation of God. The next day I was called before a concerned dean and an irate vice president, who told me about "many, many, many" telephone calls from angry parents. I was relieved of all my teaching duties, replaced by a Catholic priest with an interest in history, and given two graduate students to advise on their research.

An Opportune Time

Irene Brady Thomas

I was born at the end of 1945, still considered a "war baby." Through my school years, our class was half the size of the hordes of boomers that followed. I was comfortably tucked inside an envelope of time. This cushion contained room for growth, government money, opportunity, and less competition for space. The optimism I received from my situation remains a constant, and I consider finding the city of Alameda, California, among the richest awards I've been given.

My first husband and I lived in Hollywood, California, for seven years, following our adventurous move west with our thirteen-month-old twin girls. Chicago, my hometown, had been just a stopping point in life for my husband, who wanted to realize his dream of an acting career in Hollywood. In 1967, with our third child due, we decided to move. With $300 and no job or apartment, we set out with our two babies along the southern route to California. When we arrived we spent one night with an aunt in Hollywood, and within one day we found a furnished apartment, and Glenn found a job with United California Bank, setting up a new program called MasterCard. Life in Hollywood was never dull in the hippie era. My husband worked days and took part in small playhouse productions. The children started school in Hollywood—another stopping point and a familiar name for those seeking a new life from all around the world. I worked at my children's school as an aide for those learning English as a new language.

Glenn was working for Kaiser Steel in a small office they kept in Southern California, when Kaiser announced a consolidation of offices to their headquarters in Oakland. They gave our family a weekend to scout the Bay Area for a place to live. We were invited to the Kaiser Building to speak with those who could help us in this effort. It was suggested that we might like to live in the Walnut Creek/Concord area. I did not drive then, and I was hoping to find a place within walking distance to shopping, a library, and public transportation. Someone mentioned having parents that lived in Alameda and told us to find "the Tube" and we would be there. Well, we finally found that tube in bustling Oakland Chinatown, drove through it and, to my delight, found the answer to all of my needs. We made our way out of the dark tunnel and drove south along Webster Street, turning right onto Central Avenue at twilight. In the area were smaller homes, previously beach cottages, commingled with mid-sized Victorians and 1940s-style apartment houses. At that time, the Naval Air Station was a huge presence, and bars and shops catering to the navy lined Webster. Oblivious to this, we spent the night at the motel next to Sambo's restaurant just off the road to the base. All the noise and night traffic never bothered me, because Alameda was *it*.

We picked up a street map and explored the island. We discovered that the Gold Coast was populated by Victorian Ladies, massive homes decorated with carved wood, spindles, and eaves, painted in the wild colors of the 60s and 70s. Back in Hollywood in our small rental home, I spent hours going over that street map. First, I noticed that Alameda was completely surrounded by water. Yacht clubs seemed to line three of those coasts, boat ramps on Ballena Bay, at the Bay Farm Bridge, and along the estuary. The navy base dominated the West End. Schools seemed to be everywhere, many with public parks adjacent to them. In Hollywood I had to walk miles each day to parks where my children could play, and now it seemed that my kids would be able to walk easily to schools, parks, church, and pools. I was fascinated by the Model Airplane Field, just across the Bay Farm Bridge. Bay Farm was indeed what its name suggested. Farms covered the area. The only street occupied by homes was Maitland Drive, just beyond the public golf course. Bus service was ideal, and it seemed to me that this beautiful place was a small town, yet within only ten miles we had the opportunity to visit two major cities.

My husband was given two more paid days to travel alone to find us a place to live. He looked around and checked out the papers on his first day and on the second day, about to give up in Alameda, he drove once more through different neighborhoods, finding a nice quiet street, Alameda Avenue. There was a For Rent sign at a house on the block just before Alameda High School. He inquired, and by our good fortune secured that house for us.

By our standards this place was a mansion. Two finished floors, once broken up into possibly two apartments. It was a collection of small rooms with the downstairs containing massive large finished areas. It was as if our children had their own apartment in the rear. One of the downstairs areas became a playroom, and the front made it possible for my husband to finally set up a large train set, which had been his hobby. We had a yard in back, parking, and a driveway between our place and the Victorian with apartments next door. Young families just like us resided in these apartments, and we immediately had friends in our new city.

In the early 70s, Alameda High School shared property cut through by Alameda Avenue all the way to Park Street. One block beyond us were private homes, the school/public pool, and a synagogue. Porter School was near the corner of Oak Street and

Encinal Avenue. Unfortunately, Porter School burned down in 1973. Because of that our children had a long walk over to Lum School each day. By that time, March, 1974, our three children were in first and second grades. I remember walking them on their first day. From then on, they walked by themselves with their friends down Willow and all the way to Grand Street.

In July, we welcomed our fourth child. That summer I planted a vegetable garden. The neighborhood kids held puppet shows, did theatrical productions out our back window, and spent hours in the pool. On Saturdays they went to the free kids' matinee at the Alameda Theater.

I attended adult driving classes at the high school, taught by Mr. Hennessee. Mr. Stanford was my right-seat instructor. He was a saint, never flinching on our first drive into San Leandro and back. I was fortunate enough to take my DMV test with the high school students because I did not have a car. The test was a day of the Oakland A's world series game with the Dodgers, and traffic was so congested that we had to stay on side streets. Lucky me!

I took classes at the College of Alameda and Laney College for $3 per semester hour. Our school-age children took part in summer programs at Rittler and later Krusi and Edison parks. The Alameda Recreation and Parks Department paid for everything, including T-shirts, snacks, and softball and baseball park leagues and weekly field trips. Many of the local churches had one-week summer programs. The library also kept our Alameda children busy all summer. The Alameda Theater had summer specials: Tuesday was dollar day at the theater for everyone.

County offices on Santa Clara Avenue provided immunizations for Alameda children. There was a DMV branch on Encinal near Versailles back then.

Unfortunately, we had to move after our rental was put on the market and we could not afford the $44,000 asking price. With some help though, we were able to buy our first house, and our $226 monthly mortgage was less than our former rent. Our lucky star followed us to the corner of Broadway and Encinal. This very old house needed lots of work! A massive acacia covered the roof and when it needed to be removed, it left gaping holes in the roof. Roof and gutters came first.

We bought our home in 1975 and by 1978, that little pocket of opportunity we had found started to change, at least in our pocketbooks. We were definitely a working-class family, and in the three years between 1975 and 1978, house prices started to skyrocket, sometimes doubling because of demand. Those of us who could easily carry our mortgage payment were shocked and sorely worried when we received our tax assessments and property tax bills. Something had to be done or many of us would lose our homes. In 1978, two-thirds of homeowners passed Proposition 13, rolling back our assessed value and limiting the yearly rise of taxes.

In the early 1980s I became a single working mother with four children ranging in age from six to thirteen, living in a 1896 dilapidated white-frame house with a patched-together backyard fence that our dog would get through, and once I found myself in dog court, where I was able to avoid a fine by giving blood. That is not an option now, but the Red Cross surely benefited by Judge McDonald's rulings, and I started a habit of blood donations, which I continue to this day.

On a walk I saw a window sign: "This house is being rehabilitated by the City of Alameda." I called and was visited by a lovely woman who helped me assess my needs, and asked me how much I could afford each month on a loan. I told her I could pay one hundred per month. We needed new windows, a front and back porch, paint, carpeting, and fence. The city architect designed all the porches; the city paid three points on the 15-percent interest at that time, provided inspectors each day, and all the permits. All I had to do was pick out colors! I will be forever thankful to Alameda for this opportunity.

I mentioned the inflation that burdened so many back in the early 80s and the taxpayer revolt and Proposition 13. This law saved me from losing my home, but at the same time it triggered the loss of many of those amenities that enriched our lives in other ways. Schools and parks now had to charge for services that we had taken for granted.

Alameda was a place where navy families decided to retire and where families lived for generations. Now our youth are not able to afford to live here. This is no longer a place where working-class people can find jobs. We watch and wonder about the future. Older folks still can find fairly reasonably priced services and fun at the Mastick Senior Center, but housing is especially tenuous. I see seniors who live in their cars, waiting for housing. Lines run around the block at county housing offices. I hear of young people who may find themselves unable to pay a parking fine or misdemeanor, which sets them on a downward spiral of debt and hopelessness about the future.

I love Alameda. This city has offered me so much. So much hope. The circumstances of my birth, no doubt, offered me the best of times. I did my part too. I researched and took risks when opportunity presented itself. I wish the same for all who follow me.

LUCKY

Philip Tribuzio

While we sit at the table with a cup of tea
I'll tell you a true story all about me.
A condensed eulogy fills my head,
but that seems extreme as I'm not yet dead.
To present my character without backing,
or for things to brag about, I am lacking.
Who cares how through the years I did last
when telling of a mundane past,
except to contrast and to compare
with Mastick members who like to share.

I was born in Oakland California in 1926. I was almost adopted by my aunt at five years old, when my mother died during the great Depression. I was lucky to have a good-natured and kind father that kept his two boys with him to live on a country farm past Castro Valley, where we lived until I was eleven years old.

I never went hungry. In fact, I never had relatives, friends, or acquaintances that ever went hungry. Dad fed everybody. I remember the kitchen always smelled good. Dad gathered mustard greens and mushrooms and other things to cook but his favorite dish was spaghetti. Friends from Oakland drove to our home for the day for ``Nick's spaghetti." They brought their kids to play and often left behind their unwanted dog. The city dogs loved running wild in the country and eating leftover spaghetti. Dad would start making sauce early Saturday and let it simmer all night. We would wake up Sunday morning smelling the sauce cooking away on the wood stove. I was only four but I remember once seeing dad with a big spoon stirring spaghetti in a big washtub on an open fire outside.

Dad had a lot of friends, some he had done contracting work for before the 1929 stock market crash, and a lot of Italian friends too. They all came for spaghetti, and he enjoyed their compliments, especially about the tender chunks of meat that had simmered in tomato sauce all night. After dinner he would tell them the meat was from the Rowell horse ranch, which was past our Palamares school on the highway from Castro Valley. No matter, they came back on Sundays anyway.

Our house wasn't like the other farms. Even though it was at the end of the road, we had electricity. Some farms had outhouses, but Dad was a contractor so we had well water pumped to a tank, and we had inside plumbing like in the city. My brother and I took care of chickens and a hundred rabbits and a cow. We had live-in housekeepers. Dad tried three or four short marriages, hoping to find someone to help to watch my brother and me, but we never had a stepmother.

My big brother, Fran, and I walked a mile or so to the two-room county school. We never heard of either kindergarten or school buses. The sheep rancher's two boys rode their old horse bareback across the three-lane highway to get to school.

I was lucky my big brother protected me, and I never got into a fist fight or broke bones. I had a wise father who civilized me.

He didn't smoke or drink or swear, and I followed his example. Dad loved to pull the one-arm bandit in Reno and thought he was lucky. Even so, I learned to never gamble. Dad taught me to respect elders and not to do anything to be ashamed of, and to leave past tribulations to history.

Dad couldn't afford supporting a farm so we moved to East Oakland, where nobody locked their doors because California was the best place on earth, and I was lucky to go to good city schools.

Working construction with dad, I learned a positive work attitude. I didn't plan or have the means to waste time in college, so I was lucky to gain wisdom from years of observing others.

That calls for a tea break and a slice of the banana bread I just baked. As you can see, I'm doing just fine. Two new eyes, successful cancer operation in 2005, and Kaiser hospital constantly watching over my health needs. My father-in-law used to show his false teeth like the comic strip cartoon characters. I'm lucky to have all my teeth, well almost all, and I can chew an apple.

What else can I tell you? I was lucky to be able to drive an eighteen-wheeler till age seventy, before retiring to take care of my dearly beloved, who passed in 2003. I was a good driver, and driving big trucks and training other drivers was my profession. At my age now, I'm lucky I can still drive, and lucky my license won't expire until 2020.

Let's change the subject from expiration dates. I don't want to think of when and where or how I'll expire.

Learning about life started for me when I joined the army. I was lucky that my dad, my brother, and I didn't have to go overseas during World War Two. My brother joined the navy and I was a supernumerary in the army. My first weeks at army training camp included enemy recognition, during which the army doctor informed us about the danger of venereal disease. The doctor was very serious, telling us that even nice girls can pass it on. He warned us to look but don't touch. At eighteen I was impressed, and that's been my guide ever since.

I remember one day, at Shepherd Field Army Base in Texas, when I had guard duty. I had to wear an armband and a gun holster for an army 45, commonly called a hand cannon. It was so heavy I had to cinch up the gun belt. My job was to take four Italian military prisoners to burn trash. I recognized their Italian talk, but Dad never taught me to speak Italian because he wanted me to be American, so I didn't know what they were saying. They spoke good English too. They led me to the incinerator, and the weather was warm and dry with a light breeze, like in southern Italy they told me.

I learned from them that Italian soldiers were very unhappy in the war and surrendered in 1944 in large numbers. I was assured no one would try to escape because in fact their imprisonment in the US was a vacation compared to suffering army service in sandy Egypt. They even had their own kitchen, and they ate better than in Italy, they said.

One prisoner kept the incinerator fire going, and the others burned the trash, picking out some discarded letters from home to American soldiers. We were out of sight of the prison buildings, and as they read out loud the racy letters from soldiers' girlfriends, I gained a new outlook on the Italian prisoners, as well as on some other things.

Excitement? In high school I passed the army test for pilot training, which was exciting. I never got to fly in the army, but I was lucky to earn a pilot's license on the GI bill. Getting married was exciting. Frances married me when we were both twenty-five. I had known her since 1937, when she lived next door to my uncle.

We had a church wedding in 1951, and I had a lucky fifty years with the only girl I have ever kissed. That may be old-fashioned, but I never had need of a midlife crisis.

Another cup of tea while we compare the cultural changes from the era when the husband made the living and the wife made the living worthwhile. Frances and I didn't have children, but after fostering a few we had the excitement of adopting our baby girl in 1963 and our baby boy in 1966. I was lucky to be able to be the sole support of our family, so Frances could be home with the children.

We were lucky to keep our Alameda home all these years. I have observed families moving away from each other, and I have been lucky that my grown son stayed and takes care of me. Barry is a great son. We build things in our garage woodworking shop, and luckily we work well together without controversy.

I have a full cupboard and fridge, and I can cook spaghetti whenever I want. Luckily, living an ordinary life, I have no recriminations, no regrets, no apologies, no worries, and I am grateful for being. Just happy-go-lucky.

About the Authors

Mary Ashford

Mary was born in the UK and served in the British Foreign Service in London and Hong Kong. After moving to the US she worked in publishing in Boston for many years. She has taken creative writing workshops at the Fine Arts Workshop in Provincetown, Massachusetts, and she cofounded the Cozy Street Writers in  Cambridge, Massachusetts, in 2002. In order to live closer to her daughter and grandson, she moved to Alameda in 2013.

Janet Beatty

Janet moved to Alameda in 2003 to retire after thirty years as a Presbyterian minister. She is a master gardener and has a plot in the Bay/Eagle Community Garden. She also serves on the advisory committee for the Jean Sweeney Open Space, helping to plan a community garden, urban orchard, and demonstration garden. A member of the Mastick Senior  Center's creative writing workshop, Janet recently published a children's book, *Iris Loses Her Purple.* Her two daughters, son-in-law, and two grandchildren all live in Alameda.

Bonnie Bone

Bonnie is an Atlanta native who bounced around the country before landing in Alameda in 1986, where she has lived ever since. While she misses the sultry nights and honeyed evenings

of her beloved South, she is placated by the beauty of the Bay Area, its progressive politics, and the intriguing people she has come to know here. She hopes they forgive her for always writing about them. She lives with her two cats, Button and Sugar Pie, who are forever offering their resistance to her writing, yet are her two most loyal fans. She is currently working on a novel.

Janet Brown

Janet and her family have lived in Alameda for forty-five years. Her son attended kindergarten at Mastick School one year before Mastick Senior Center was founded there. The center feels like a home away from home for her. In her spare time Janet likes to sew, do needlework, socialize, eat out, dance, and go thrift shopping.

Shirley S. Daguman

Shirley is also known as Lee, and was born in the Philippines. At the age of two, after her sister was born, Lee and her mother and baby sister came to the US, where her dad was in the navy. Lee grew up in San Francisco. She is an artist and self-taught floral and fashion designer, designing and making wearable art, and has recently become an acrylic painter as well. She is also a registered dental assistant with a degree in nutrition. A Mastick member since 2015, Lee is a volunteer instructor of the beading jewelry class at Mastick.

Pierrette Dick-Moore

Pierrette has lived in Alameda since 2010. In addition to California and Colorado she has resided in New Jersey, Texas, Oregon, and New Mexico. Pierrette's career included being the owner-manager of a restaurant in Denver, a manager of travel agencies in Houston and Sacramento, a member of the corporate staff of a large regional travel agency in Oakland, and most recently a court-appointed advocate for children living in foster homes.

Karren Lutz Elsbernd

Karren once again lives in Oakland, where in the 1960s she graduated from the California College of Arts and Crafts. In the following years she lived and raised her two children in San Francisco while continuing academic studies in the humanities along with creative pursuits including painting and the quilt arts. Karren started her career as a volunteer

in the special collections department of the California Academy of Sciences. She was soon hired onto the staff of their natural history research library, and retired after twenty years with the title of Library Assistant of Archives and Digital Collections.

Isabella Gussoni Fahrney

Isabella was born in Padova, Italy, and grew up in Rome. She immigrated to California in 1960 and moved to Alameda in 1990. She

has two children, Barbara and David, and three grandchildren, Zachary, Madeline, and Christian. In her varied career Isabella was a salesperson, a travel consultant/tour guide, a DJ for an Italian radio program, and an importer. Tennis, sailing, and travel used to be her hobbies; she still travels, but gardening, reading, writing, movies, and history are now her main interests.

Sally Faulhaber

Sally was born in Berkeley a few months before the Great Crash. She returned in 1957 for graduate study at UC Berkeley. In 1968

she and her husband, Bill, moved to Alameda to be within easy cycling distance of his job at the Naval Air Station. Their daughters Susannah and Lisa were born there and attended Alameda schools. Sally's climbing, hiking, and skiing have long since been replaced with knitting, quilting, and walking her dog. She is still involved with the League of Women Voters.

Nell Fliehmann

Nell, who celebrated her ninety-fifth birthday October 5, 2017, lives in Oakland in an apartment with stunning views over Lake Merritt. Two years ago she wrote and published a book, *Born to Travel: Stories of My Life and Travels,* and since then has replaced writing with painting.

Catherine Folsom

Catherine is a native of Alameda, and is married to Noel Folsom. She has three children, Christopher, Timothy, and Michael, and two grandchildren, Keona and Matthew. Before retirement she was the office manager at St. Barnabas Catholic Church, and she enjoys gardening, opera, ballet, and jigsaw puzzles.

Noel Folsom

Noel is a retired US Army major, and has degrees from San Francisco State University, Golden Gate University, and a diploma from the US Army Command and General Staff School. After his military service he worked as the agency planner for the Alameda County Social Services Agency. Noel and his wife, Cathy,

have three sons, Christopher, Timothy, and Michael; and two grandchildren, Keona and Matthew. Noel enjoys bridge, photography, military history, and paddle-wheel boat trips with Cathy.

Bob Frank

Bob believed Horace Greeley's advice, "Go West, young man," applied to him, and moved to California in 2014. He has been a resident of Alameda since June 2016, and enjoys having retired here more than had he retired anywhere else. At one time Bob lived near the Grand Canyon of the East; now he lives near the onetime Coney Island of the West.

Oliver Guinn, PhD

Oliver taught undergraduate economics for thirty-five years at Washburn University in Topeka, Kansas, where he also served as associate dean. He then spent ten years as a financial analyst with the US Department of Education, Student Financial Aid.

Stanley Hallmark

Stanley regards himself as a true Alamedan. (His youngest aunt called herself a CIO, a California Improved Okie.) He was born in Oklahoma and came to California in 1943 with his parents when his father took a job at the Richmond Shipyards. Stanley was raised and educated in the Bay Area, resulting in a BS, a BA, and an MA. He has a daughter and granddaughter who also live in Alameda, and he is a fixture at

the small newspaper booth on the corner of Park Street and Santa Clara, dispensing wisdom and change with equal authority, and generally livening things up.

Paul Hauser

Paul was a construction/facility executive with forty-five years of experience in the pub-lic-private sector and served on many notable non-profit boards. He was a former deco-rated U.S. Air Force officer. Paul and his wife moved to Alameda in 2012 to be near their son and daughter-in-law and three grandchil-dren. In addition to being the author of four published works, Paul currently serves as the president of the Mastick Senior Center advisory board. The inspira-tion for this book grew from Paul's interest in seniors' stories.

Usha Muliyil Helm

Usha was born in Mysore, India, and has lived in the Bay Area for twenty-three years. Her major interests are writing and working for social jus-tice. She is grateful to have the opportunity to share her story.

Virginia Leung Jang

Virginia a native of Hong Kong, is a long-time resident of California. After retirement, she and her husband moved to Alameda in 2004. Virginia enjoys world travel, and on most days you can find her at Mastick's exer-cise classes and afternoon social bridge. She hopes one day she will finish the writing she started in 2000, about her travels and eating Chinese food on different continents.

Mary-Jo P. Knight

Lives with Mike Parish in Alameda and is the proud grandma of

Tohaana and Alowaan Johns. She sings with the Oakland Symphony Chorus and is a member of the 9-Holers at Chuck Corica Golf Complex. US Route 80 is about as far from Alameda on the West Coast as it was from her New York home on the East Coast, end to end.

Henry Long

Henry has resided in Alameda since 1986. After a long career in social work in the developmental disability field, he retired in October 2016. Henry enjoys tennis, bicycling, and camping in the Sierra. He is currently writing his life story for his son.

Christine Rose Lyons

Christine was born in Poland. After immigrating to Israel, she

moved to London, New York, and finally to Los Angeles. Beginning in Hollywood in the 1970s, she was a freelance writer, translator, and editorial portfolio and art photographer. Christine and Richard Lyons were married in 1978, moved to Berkeley in 1979, and to Alameda in 1988. Christine has particularly enjoyed being part of the active community of artists and writers living and working in Alameda.

Ros McIntosh

Ros hails from Europe. She fondly remembers Germany, England, France, and Massachusetts (where she studied), but she wouldn't trade Alameda for any place. Walking on the beach, bicycling to bridge games and classes at Mastick, playing the piano, writing books, and skiing are her beloved pastimes.

J. Michael Parish

Michael is a retired Wall Street attorney who now lives in Alameda with his partner, Mary-Jo Knight. Mike collects art photography, and enjoys visiting museums, tending his roses, and writing, and has published a number of short stories and won some poetry prizes. He also enjoys taking his granddaughters, Alowaan and Tohaana, to Golden Gate Fields Race Track and making sure they win money on every visit.

Gwendolyn (Spratley) Pirack

Gwendolyn was born in Oakland and has resided in Alameda ever since. She studied fine arts and started out as a commercial artist, and then earned her teaching credential and taught for sixteen years and substituted for fourteen after retirement. She has also

been a Bible study leader. As an athlete, Gwen won medals and trophies in 5K running and tennis. She plays Scrabble and learned to play bridge at Mastick, where she had been a teacher's aide back when Mastick was an elementary school.

Elizabeth Prosser

Elizabeth is a former social worker. She lives in Alameda, where she writes articles for her homeowners' association community newsletter, walks her Yorkshire terrier, Teddy, and takes classes at Mastick.

Trudie Schierenbeck

Trudie was born in Germany and immigrated to the US to marry after World War II. She has two children. After her husband's death in 1996, Trudie spent time traveling with friends. She has been a member of the Alameda Poets and a member of Mastick for thirty years, where she's taken ceramics classes and now writes memoir, short stories, and poetry in the creative writing workshop.

Miriam Schiffman

Miriam moved from Boston, Massachusetts, to California in 1952, when she was thirteen years old. She graduated from Oakland High School and the University of California. She and Stan, her high school sweetheart, spent forty years back East, where Miriam earned her masters in social work, worked, and raised their two children. In 2001 she and Stan retired to Alameda. Life is now filled with theater, travel, sculling, and learning. Miriam enjoys Mastick Senior Center, where she has served on the board and takes classes in bridge and creative writing.

Joe Shahpar

Joe was born in a land known for outstanding literature and grew up appreciating the nuances of the Persian prose and poetry. At high school in Iran he was the editor for the student literary magazine. In the US, where he's been living for more than sixty years, he has gravitated toward English literature, and although he still writes in Persian, he dreams of becoming another Joseph Conrad, writing in his second language. A resident of Alameda for forty years, he is following his dream at the Mastick Senior Center's writing workshop.

Bill Soares

Bill is an Alameda native and unmarried at this time.

Gayle Southworth

Gayle has been an Alameda resident for several decades and taught at a number of universities, in addition to his efforts involving human rights. He has been a Dodgers fan since childhood, since the Dodgers, from their Brooklyn days, broadcast their games on the radio in the very upper Midwest, including the Dakotas, where very little else was going on.

Irene Brady Thomas

Irene was born in Chicago, and moved to Alameda in 1974. After years of raising children and attending art classes, she shared an art studio on Oakland Embarcadero. She financed her former art business by working at the Spectator Bookstore on Park Street, and worked later as an aide at the Alameda Library. She is currently a volunteer library aide at Mastick Senior Center.

Phil Tribuzio

Phil, when in and around Mastick Senior Center, is recognized by his beret and his walker. He attends the creative writing workshop every Tuesday, to join with other writers of essays, stories, and poems. Phil has five self-published stories in the Mastick library and is working now on his life story for a great-grandchild curious to read about how Great-Granddad lived in the old days.

Acknowledgments

The prospect of inviting thirty-two seniors to write stories about their life experiences was daunting as well as exciting. A Mastick Senior Center book committee was formed early on, to encourage people to participate and assist them in completing the project.

Book committee members that so graciously provided their time and talent were: Sally Faulhaber, Robert Frank, Paul Hauser, Carrie Pickett, Gwen Pirack, Kristine Watson, and Jerry Yarbrough. Joseph Woodard Multimedia photographed the contributors. Robert Frank came up with the idea for the book cover. Clayton J. Mitchell Photography provided the book cover design, and Berkshire Hathaway Home Services, Drysdale Properties provided the book cover aerial photograph. Carrie Pickett helped writers bring their work into final form. Financial support for this book was provided by Comfort Keepers Home Care of Alameda. Jackie Krause, Mastick Senior Center Recreation Manager, and her staff provided the resources and encouragement to help see this unique project through.

A special thanks to all the writers for sharing something of their life stories.

CPSIA information can be obtained
at www.ICGtesting.com
Printed in the USA
FSHW021956071119
63883FS